University of Cambridge

Department of Applied Economics

OCCASIONAL PAPERS

3

The Economies of Large-scale Production in British Industry

An Introductory Study

by C. PRATTEN and R. M. DEAN

in collaboration with A. SILBERSTON

CAMBRIDGE UNIVERSITY PRESS

Price 15s. net; $3.00

Economists have long known about the potential advantages of large-scale production but have done relatively
little empirical work on the subject. In this introductory
study the authors discuss problems associated with the
measurement of economies of large-scale production,
and present four case studies on book printing, footwear
manufacture, the steel industry and oil refining. Their
conclusions fill many gaps in our knowledge of the factors affecting the efficient working of British industries.
They should be studied by all who seek to make British
industry competitive in the markets of the world.

The research on which this study is based was carried
out in the Department of Applied Economics, Cambridge.
A similar study is being prepared on a further group of
industries.

University of Cambridge

Department of Applied Economics

OCCASIONAL PAPERS 3

THE ECONOMIES OF
LARGE-SCALE PRODUCTION IN BRITISH INDUSTRY
An Introductory Study

The Economies of Large-scale Production in British Industry

An Introductory Study

by C. PRATTEN and R. M. DEAN
in collaboration with A. SILBERSTON

 CAMBRIDGE
at the UNIVERSITY PRESS
1965

PUBLISHED BY

THE SYNDICS OF THE CAMBRIDGE UNIVERSITY PRESS

Bentley House, 200 Euston Road, London, N. W. 1

American Branch: 32 East 57th Street, New York, N. Y. 10022

West African Office: P. O. Box 33, Ibadan, Nigeria

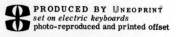 PRODUCED BY UNEOPRINT
set on electric keyboards
photo-reproduced and printed offset

at The Gresham Press
UNWIN BROTHERS LIMITED
Old Woking Surrey England

Contents

LIST OF TABLES

Preface

Economists have long written about the economies of large-scale production, and every economics textbook has a section on the subject. Very few, however, give any quantitative notion of how important these economies are in any particular industry. In recent years economists have been giving increasing attention to measuring economies of scale partly because it has been realised that rational decisions—about whether or not to join the European Common Market, and whether or not to pass legislation restraining mergers, for example—cannot be made without more information than we yet have. We have certainly felt in the Department of Applied Economics that a good deal more work needs to be done on economies of scale before there is a sufficient background of knowledge to enable economists to advise policy makers adequately. Mainly at the suggestion of Professor E. A. G. Robinson, who has himself written on the subject, a research project on economies of scale was commenced in the Department of Applied Economics. The work has been under my general supervision but the detailed research was carried out by Mr. R. M. Dean, before he took up a post in the Planning Commission in Ghana, and by Mr. C. Pratten. We have throughout had the benefit of advice from Professor E. A. G. Robinson and from Mr. W. B. Reddaway, the Director of the Department of Applied Economics.

This Occasional Paper represents the first fruits of our research. We deal with general concepts in the first chapter, present four detailed studies of industries, and sum up in a final chapter. Mr. R. M. Dean was responsible for the original work on book-printing and the steel industry and Mr. C. Pratten for the original work on footwear and oil refining. Since Mr. Dean left us, Mr. Pratten has extensively revised the chapters on book printing and steel in the light of further information that we have received.

Research of this nature requires detailed knowledge and the collection of a considerable quantity of data. It makes particularly heavy demands on industry for information. In the course of the research we have had to visit a large number of firms and institutions and we would like to express here our great gratitude to all those who have helped us. We have done our best to be accurate over the technical and other details of the industries we have studied, and our industry chapters have been vetted by those with experience in the industries concerned. We are, however, solely responsible for any errors or misconceptions which remain.

We call this an introductory study because we have already started work on a further group of industries. Our present intention is to embody the results of the research on this new group of industries, together with the research results given in this Paper, in a book on economies of scale to be published in the not too distant future. In that work we hope to be able to say more about the implications of our research than we have been able to do in this Occasional Paper, and also to take advantage of comments arising out of this interim Paper to improve our final product.

University of Cambridge   A. S.
Department of Applied Economics

February 1965

The Meaning and Measurement of the Economies of Scale

An Outline of the Project

This paper is a progress report on a project of research being undertaken at the Department of Applied Economics to measure and compare
the economies of large-scale production in a number of industries. So
far we have studied four industries, book printing, footwear manufacture,
steel production and oil refining and have described these studies in this
paper. But first we discuss the meaning of economies of scale and the
methods of measuring these economies.

For a plant or firm making a homogeneous product the scale of production can be measured by the number of units produced per unit of time,
and the economies of scale for such plants are the potential reductions
in average unit costs of production associated with higher levels of productive capacity. In practice most plants and firms manufacture a range
of products because it is cheaper to make products jointly, or because
demand is insufficient to allow specialisation, or because specialisation
on one product is regarded as too risky. For multi-product plants and
firms scale is a multi-dimensional concept. The scale of production may
be changed not only by altering the overall capacity to produce more of
all products, or more of some products only, but also in other ways, such
as by altering the length of production runs or the extent of standardisation.
In this study we have attempted to make a comprehensive assessment of
the economies of scale for the industries we have studied and for this
purpose we have considered the relationships between unit costs and all
the main dimensions of scale, as described in more detail below.

Discussion by economists of the forces determining the economies of
scale and the optimum size for business units can be traced back to
Adam Smith's description of the importance of the division of labour for
efficiency. One purpose of the project is to provide additional empirical
backing for the theoretical discussion by economists of the economies of
scale. We have attempted to make a detailed assessment of the overall
economies of scale, and the relative importance of the various forces
determining these economies, for the industries which we have studied.

Another purpose of the project is to provide information which will throw
some light on the results of government economic policy which, inten-
tionally or incidentally, affects the scale of production. Examples of such
government intervention are the regulations governing monopolies, tax
concessions to small firms, government pressure to rationalise industries, and incentives to firms to set up new factories in development
areas. In many under-developed countries, governments exercise considerable influence in determining which industries are to be set up, and

the economies of scale are one of the factors which should be considered in making such decisions. One of the arguments used to support policies designed to reduce tariff barriers is that the expanded markets so provided will reduce unit production costs because of the economies of scale Co-operative schemes and mergers of firms to reduce costs of production are advocated, and politicians and economists debate the merits of nationalisation and higher rates of growth for the economy. Decisions on all these matters, which affect the scale of production in the short or long term, have to be taken at present mainly on the basis of impressionistic evidence as to the results of a change in the scale of production on unit costs. It is hoped that an assessment of the economies of scale in a selection of industries will be useful for administrators faced with decisions in these fields, and that it will be possible at a later stage of the project to make a general assessment of the effects of an increase in the scale of production on economic efficiency for broad categories of industry.

Definition of Economies of Scale

1. Single-product firms

Though the phrase 'economies of scale' has often been used both in economic literature and elsewhere it is necessary to define clearly what we are attempting to measure. In the past, the use of the phrase 'economies of scale', especially in economics textbooks, has usually been considered in relation to plants producing a single standard product, and for such plants the meaning of the phrase is apparently straightforward. Economies of scale are the potential reductions in average unit costs which are associated with higher levels of productive capacity, with capacity measured in terms of the number of units of the standard product which can be produced per unit of time.

If it were possible to make experiments to determine economic relationships, then, to determine the economies of scale for an industry, plants would be designed and set up to produce the single standard product at varying levels of output, and comparisons would be made between the unit costs of production for these plants. Each plant would be designed to produce a certain output at the lowest possible cost, and all other conditions except the level of output and the consequences flowing from this condition would be held constant. From the operating data for such plants it would be possible to estimate the long run average cost curve for the industry, i.e. the curve showing the lowest possible cost of producing at any scale of output when all possible adaptation to that scale of output had taken place.(1)

Technical knowledge and relative factor prices are examples of the conditions which would be held constant. This would not require the same

---

(1) This is the well-known 'envelope' curve of long run average costs, first discussed by Jacob Viner in Zeitschrift für Nationalökonome, Vol. 111, 1931-1, pp. 23-46, and reprinted in The Long View and the Short by Jacob Viner, 1958.

techniques to be used at all plants, but that the optimum techniques would be selected for each plant and would be chosen from a known set of techniques. As the scale of plants increased the techniques selected would probably alter. For example, at low levels of capacity, batch production is the most effective method of organising the production of motor cars, whereas at higher levels of capacity flow production methods, and the use of automatic transfer equipment, reduce the costs of production. The concept of a set of techniques is to some extent unreal because technical progress is taking place continuously and, if it was decided to build plants of a different scale than hitherto, this would itself almost certainly lead to technical developments. In principle, however, we try to abstract from this when studying economies of scale.

Variations in relative factor prices may also effect the optimum method of production. For example, in the footwear industry one of the forces determining whether it is cheaper to cut leather by press or by hand is the relationship between the wages of 'clickers' and the price of presses. Our estimates of economies of scale are based on the existing structure of wages and prices in this country. They cannot therefore be assumed to apply to other countries with different relative factor prices. However we shall show that the costs of operating capital equipment form a surprisingly small proportion of costs in two of the industries we have studied and that in the other two industries the scope for substituting labour for capital is technically limited for most processes. So our conclusions would probably apply for many other countries even if relative factor prices there were appreciably different.

Total costs for each plant, from which costs per unit of output could be derived, would include the cost of materials and services bought out, wages and salaries, a charge for depreciation(1) and for interest on capital employed. The economies of scale would be measured by the percentage reduction in unit costs as scale increased and this relationship could be determined both for unit costs as a whole and for the components of these costs, e.g. labour and capital costs. For such an analysis, costs could alternatively be broken down for each of the various types of production process used. If unit costs are a minimum at a certain level of capacity or range of capacity, this would be the 'optimum scale' of production. If unit costs at first fall as scale increases, and then level off, the point at which they level off would be the 'minimum optimum scale' of output. The extent of the fall of unit costs and the speed of the fall as scale increases is important for determining the significance of economies of scale in relation to other forces influencing efficiency in the industry concerned.

In passing we may note that, even if we could set up plants in this way to

---

(1) Wherever possible in the course of our studies we have based estimates of depreciation on estimated replacement costs of assets and have used the straight line method of depreciation commonly employed by accountants. Depreciation thus calculated often gives only a rough approximation of the actual rate of capital consumption in any particular period.

determine the economies of scale, there would in practice be some complications. A problem of definition could occur because plants designed to produce at some levels of capacity may perform operations which, at other levels of capacity, it would be cheaper to buy out. If the scope of the operations performed at plants varies according to scale in this way, another dimension of scale, the number of operations performed, is introduced. The relationship between average unit costs and the level of output, measured in terms of final units produced, no longer gives a comprehensive measure of the economies of scale, although this relationship is still, of course, of interest.

Another problem which could arise in practice is that important factors of production cannot be held constant. For example, if we were measuring the economies of scale for coal mining it would be impossible to set up mines with differing levels of output but with identical coal seam conditions. A more general factor, which it might be difficult to hold constant, is manpower. This could vitiate comparisons where the quality of the labour force can significantly affect costs, for example in industries where the efficiency of the individual employee is important and where the ability of management can have a decisive influence on this efficiency.

It may not in practice be possible to make an immediate assessment of the costs of plants of varying capacity because of the 'learning effect'. It takes some time for plants to be worked up to full efficiency, because personnel need to obtain experience of operating plant and take time to acquire skills. In practice, methods of production are usually subject to continuous improvement, though this often involves the introduction of at least some additional capital and the use of new techniques. It is conceivable that the learning effect and the prospects for development may be greater for some sizes of plant than for others, and any comparisons of unit costs for plants of varying size might therefore depend upon the point in time when measurements of costs were made. The time dimension of output and the learning effect are more important if a range of products is made, and particularly if the range changes over time.

Also in practice the costs of various sizes of plant will in part be determined by the size of units which have been built in the past. Experience of building certain sizes of plant tends to reduce construction costs. Once experience of building plants of a certain size is obtained, smaller allowances for uncertainties are required, and research and development is directed at improving the performance of plants of this size. Hence estimates of economies of scale may in practice be related to the existing structure of the industry, and may not give an accurate guide to the effect of radically changing the scale of production.

There are also problems involved in the measurement of total costs. The selection of a rate of interest, which must to some extent be arbitrary, will affect comparisons if the ratio of capital employed to other inputs varies. Estimates of the life of plant which are needed to estimate depreciation are also likely to be subject to substantial margins of error, particularly if there are likely to be technical advances in the industry. Though there is no reason to expect this margin of error to be a function of the size of plants, it may affect the comparisons if capital intensity varies with scale.

14

2. Multi-product plants and firms

In practice, a range of products is manufactured by most firms, often at more than one plant. Two types of multi-product plant can be distinguished. First, those involving the joint production of two or more products for which common processes or operations are required, for example the production of coal gas and coke. Alternatively, or in addition, the production of a range of products may result from insufficient demand for particular products. For example, in the book-printing industry no firm can set up a printing-house to print one title, and similarly in the footwear industry no firm can set up a factory to manufacture one size or one style of shoe.

For multi-product plants there are several inter-related dimensions of scale which affect unit costs of production, apart from their total output. A manufacturer may be able to vary the range of products made or the length of time between revisions of his range of products; for example, a motor-car manufacturer can vary the number of models he manufactures and the interval between changing his range. In deciding the range of products to be made a manufacturer will also determine the degree of standardisation. One type of standardisation is the use of identical parts for distinct products, for example motor manufacturers sometimes use a common engine for two or more models. Another way of standardising output is to limit the range of products made, for example a book-printer may standardise his production by concentrating on a certain type or size of book.

The number of distinct products made by a manufacturer will also be one of the factors determining the average length of production run, i.e. the number of units of a distinct product processed before switching to the processing of another product. There are other factors determining the average length of these runs—the ability to forecast sales of products, the availability of finance and space for stocks, the possibilities for making customers wait for delivery, and the economies to be obtained by long production runs. The length of production runs may in turn have an influence on the organisation of production. The complexity of organising production, of ensuring that the right parts are available at the right place at the right time, and the losses caused by hold-ups in production, increase with the range of products made and the number of production runs. One way of reducing the range of products made on a particular production line, and of lengthening production runs in terms of time taken, is to set up additional production lines.

There is another factor which has to be taken into account. 'First copy' or design and development costs are related to the total output of the particular product to which they refer, independently of the time over which that total output is spread (and so of the output per unit of time). Some first copy costs may also be related to the number of products made, i.e. there may be economies of scale for designing and developing several products.

When estimating these relationships it is possible to assume that, for some industries, the capacity of plants can be enlarged without extending the range of products made. This applies to power stations, for example.

For other industries, such as book-printing, this assumption is not plausible. A firm in the book-printing industry cannot in general expect to increase the average size of its printing orders for titles if it expands its output capacity, and if we are considering the relationship between the size of a printing-house and unit costs of production, we can assume that the average number of copies of each title printed is not affected by output capacity. On the other hand, if an estimate of the effect of an increase in the output of the book-printing industry on unit printing costs is required, it is necessary to consider whether the average size of printing order is likely to be affected, and if so what effect this will have on printing costs.

The forces determining the economies of scale thus depend on which aspects of scale we are interested in. If we are to fulfil the objects of our project we have to obtain information which will enable us to answer such questions as:

'What is the relationship between the average unit costs of production and the output of a plant or firm?' and 'What is the effect on average unit costs of increasing the output of an industry?' It is clear that if we are to be able to answer these questions we have to estimate a number of relationships for each industry. These may include all or some of the following relationships between average unit costs of production and:

1. The length of production runs.
2. The number of distinct products made.
3. The extent of standardisation.
4. The capacity of production lines within plants.
5. The output capacity of plants and—where products are made simultaneously as in oil refining—the various possible permutations of output capacity and the extent of flexibility between various permutations of products.
6. The range of operations performed at a plant.
7. The output capacity of firms.
8. The output capacity of the industry.

In addition to considering these relationships individually we have to consider the interactions between them. We also have to consider changes in the relationships through time. For example in the case of a multi-product firm one relationship which may have to be considered in this way is that between the size of a firm and its adaptability in changing its products to meet changes in market requirements—in this connexion, small and flexible may be better than large and inflexible. In practice, although we should have liked to obtain quantitative information for all the relationships, where applicable, for the industries we have studied, this has not always been done. In some cases we have exercised a degree of selection over the relationships which we have measured because their importance varies in different industries and we wished to concentrate on the most important ones. In other cases we did not measure relationships simply because we were unable to obtain data from firms.

In the remainder of this paper, when we refer to 'the economies of scale' for an industry, we use the term to refer to the relationships between unit costs and all the dimensions of output which are applicable to the industry. The exact relationships applicable to the industry will be clear from the context.

The forces determining economies of scale

We do not propose to describe the forces determining the economies of scale in detail because there has been a great deal of discussion about these forces in the literature.(1) Nevertheless we think it necessary to describe the sources of economies of scale briefly because this is particularly important if the engineering approach(2) to measuring these economies is used. We list the forces separately below though they are, of course, inter-related.

1. Indivisibilities

There are two groups of costs which are to some extent independent of the level of output, first copy or research and development costs associated with new products, and the costs of indivisible factors of production. The first copy costs of writing and editing a newspaper are an example of the first type of indivisible costs, and the greater the number of copies of a newspaper sold the lower will be the average first copy costs. Similarly in aircraft and computer production, the cost of design and development have to be spread over the number of each type made. Analogous with first copy costs there may be first product costs which can be spread over additional products, for example a salesman may be able to sell two or more products at little if any greater cost than one product.

Many types of capital equipment are in practice indivisible. For example, presses for stamping metal parts and many machines used in the manufacture of footwear have a fixed minimum capacity. A relatively small firm is likely to be at a disadvantage when employing such machinery because it may not be able to employ it to full capacity.

---

(1) For a comprehensive discussion of the forces determining the economies of scale the reader is referred to The Structure of Competitive Industry by E. A. G. Robinson. London 1958.

(2) The engineering approach to measuring economies of scale is described on page 19. Unless engineering estimates are based on an awareness of the various sources of economies of scale they will not reflect these economies fully.

2. The economies of increased dimensions

For many types of capital equipment cost increases less rapidly than capacity. A typical example of such economies occurs in the construction of tanks. If the thickness of the walls of a tank are not affected by its size, then at least over a range of capacity the cost of increasing the capacity increases approximately in proportion to the surface area while the capacity of the tank rises in proportion to its cubic capacity.

3. The economies of specialisation

The larger the output of a product, plant, or firm, the greater will be the opportunities for specialisation of both the labour force and capital equipment. Increased output will provide greater opportunities for specialisation not only within a plant but also for suppliers of materials and services bought out.

4. The economies of massed resources

The operation of the law of large numbers may result in economies of massed resources. For example, a plant using several identical machines will have to stock proportionately fewer spare parts than a plant with only one, because it can assume that the machines will not all develop the same faults at the same time. Another example of the advantage of massed resources is that a firm operating in a number of industries, and producing a wide range of products, may benefit from the cross fertilisation of ideas and experience between its various divisions.

5. Superior organisation of production

Increased capacity may make it possible to use more efficient methods of organising production, for example as output capacity rises it may be possible to substitute methods of flow production for batch production.

6. The learning effect

Experience of manufacturing a product leads to improvements in the efficiency of production and to reductions in unit costs e.g. because there are less rejects or breakages. For example, in the footwear industry the speed at which operatives perform operations increases, and the reliability of their work improves, with their experience on particular styles. To measure the relationship between scale and output for plants, it is usually not sufficient to take a snap shot view of costs. The relationship between costs and the total output of products over time has to be considered and the learning effect is a force making for economies of long sustained output of an unchanged product.

So much for the forces contributing to the economies of scale. What are the forces which tend to limit the optimum output for products, plants, firms and industries? The clearest limitation on output is usually that imposed by the size of the market: the reduction in price or the increase in selling or transport costs required to increase sales may prevent the achievement of the full technical economies of scale. The cost of management per unit of output may increase with scale and set a limit to the optimum scale for plants or firms. As scale increases it is possible that the costs of co-ordination rise more than proportionately, and the operation of 'Parkinson's Law'—the unnecessary proliferation of staff as size increases—may affect large as compared with small firms.

The measurement of economies of scale

We have already described some of the conceptual difficulties involved in measuring the economies of scale even if we could build new plants of varying scale for the purpose of our estimates. In practice, of course, this is not possible. There are two main alternatives. Either we can compare the performance of existing plants, or we can with the aid of experts estimate the costs of production for hypothetical plants of varying scale. We have used the latter method, which we describe below. In an appendix to this chapter we discuss our reasons for rejecting other methods of measuring economies of scale.

A method of deriving the production functions of economic theory, and hence the economies of scale, from engineering production functions which describe the processes of production, has been outlined and illustrated by H. B. Chenery.(1) He used as an example the relationship between throughput capacity and costs for pipelines and derived the engineering production functions from physical and chemical laws, from experiments and from past experience. The engineering production functions related physical variables such as the diameter of a pipe, the initial and outlet pressures, and the capacity of a pipeline to transport gas. The costs of inputs, which have to be introduced to derive cost functions from engineering production functions were, in the case Chenery used, based on past experience and assumptions about the combined level of interest rates, depreciation and obsolescence.

In the studies described below the engineering approach to estimating the economies of scale has been used extensively. Methods of production have been broken down into individual processes and operations wherever possible, and the technical basis for economies of scale investigated. Unfortunately it is rare that processes can be expressed as engineering production functions which are based on scientific laws or experimental data, and so we have had to base our estimates—of the economies of scale for machines, process units and operations—on engineers', cost accountants' and managers' estimates of costs. We have also obtained capital costs and operating data for individual units of varying size and the prices quoted for machines of varying capacity. Using this type of information for the various processes etc. employed in the industries studied, we have built up estimates of the costs of production, and estimated the relationships between unit costs and the various dimensions of scale.

In some cases we have short-circuited this process by making use of estimates of the economies of scale already prepared by other people using similar methods. This has been the case particularly for our studies of the steel and oil refining industries. The preparation of

---

(1) H.B.Chenery, Q.J.E. Engineering Production Functions, November 1949.

detailed estimates of the costs for plants of varying size for these industries requires a considerable knowledge of technology, and the cost of having detailed estimates specially prepared would have been prohibitive. Firms sometimes make studies of costs for plants of varying size when planning to build a new plant, and it has been possible to obtain estimates of this type from some steel and oil companies. In addition, we have asked businessmen for estimates of the economies of scale in their industries and we have also asked them to comment on our own estimates. Their replies were based on engineering-type assessments of costs, operating experience for plants of varying size, the results of expanding plant capacity, and general experience of their industries.

The weakness of these methods of estimating economies of scale are that the estimates are subject to a margin of error and that they lack rigour. The accuracy of these methods is particularly suspect when dealing with some of the non-technical forces determining the economies of scale e.g. when estimating the relationship between size and the costs of administration. The main advantage of the engineering approach is that it enables us to hold other conditions, such as the state of the arts, the quality of factors of production, and their relative prices, constant when making estimates. In spite of its limitations we have relied heavily on the engineering approach because we consider that it is the most satisfactory method of making estimates of the economies of scale for the industries we have studied. A leading American expert in this field, Professor J. S. Bain, also relied on similar methods to estimate the economies of scale for 20 industries.(1)

The industries studied

Two of the industries, book-printing and footwear manufacture, which we selected for this initial study are relatively small-scale labour-intensive industries and the other two, steel production and oil refining, are capital intensive industries dominated by plants and firms of the largest scale. We expected that these industries would provide some interesting contrasts.

In each of the four industries, plants and firms manufacture a range of products. In the book-printing and footwear industries this is of considerable importance for a consideration of the economies of scale. For a printer each title is a separate product and a printer often prints all the copies of a title which are printed at any one time. In the footwear industry most manufacturers specialise but nevertheless make a range of styles, fittings and sizes. In both these industries we studied the relationship between the range of products and unit costs in detail.

Steel plants and oil refineries also produce a range of products, but, whereas the range of books printed by a printer is continuously changing and styles of footwear continuously evolve, the product range for firms in the steel and oil industries is relatively constant, though new products are developed and the product-mix fluctuates from time to time. For

---

(1) J. S. Bain, Barriers to New Competition. Cambridge, Mass. 1956.

both the steel and oil industries we have concentrated our attention on the overall size of plants rather than on the relationships between unit costs and the range of products made.

Appendix to Chapter 1
Alternative methods of measuring economies of scale

1. Cost comparisons

In the past, many attempts have been made to estimate the economies of scale by comparing the costs of production for existing plants. Caleb Smith and Milton Friedman have already described the difficulties involved in this approach and the former has reviewed some of the existing empirical studies.[1]

Only if the plants or firms compared make a homogeneous product is it possible to compare output in terms of the number of units produced. But if plants and firms do not make a single homogeneous product, and usually they do not, the only measures of output which can be used are total revenue or an estimate of output based on some other weighting system. Market imperfections, such as the existence of goodwill, the ownership of retail outlets, and specialisation in types, qualities and price ranges, from which it is difficult for a manufacturer to change quickly, make comparisons based on the use of total revenue as a measure of scale questionable. An example of an alternative weighting system is to revalue sales of all plants in terms of the estimated costs of production at one plant. The drawbacks to such a weighting system are that it is likely to involve the use of judgements which may be inaccurate, and that it is usually impossible to obtain the detailed information required to make such calculations.

There are also difficulties involved in the measurement of costs. One definition of total costs is that they are equal to total revenue and that profits (included in revenue) are the return on enterprise. But if we are also using total revenue to measure scale this definition cannot, of course, be used. Alternatively, we can make a notional charge for capital employed and assume that this, together with the salaries of managers, includes the remuneration of the entrepreneurial skill employed. Many qualifications and difficulties are however involved in the measurement of costs from actual data:

1. If plants were built at different dates it will be necessary to revalue capital expenditure to correct for price changes which have occurred over time.

2. Adjustments will have to be made for changes in the state of the arts and in relative factor prices. Both will have affected the techniques of

---

(1) 'Survey on the Empirical Evidence on Economies of Scale' in Business Concentration and Price Policy, Princeton, 1955, by Caleb Smith with a comment by Milton Friedman.

production used at plants built at different dates, and satisfactory adjustments may not be possible.

3. The costs of production for plants may vary for reasons not directly related to scale, for example, the uneven distribution of technical knowledge and of efficiency, the existence of patents, and differences in prices paid for similar goods and services in different regions. Even if such differences in techniques used and costs are not related to size, they make for random variations which may make it difficult to obtain reliable estimates of the relationships between output and costs from a limited number of observations. In any case, some of the differences are likely to be related to size. Newer plants tend to be larger—engineers like to obtain experience on small-scale plants first and then gradually increase the size of plants built. In addition, relatively efficient managers are likely to be in control of the larger plants and their salaries are unlikely fully to reflect this.

In view of the difficulties of measuring economies of scale by comparing costs and scale for various sizes of plant, we have not attempted to collect such data direct from firms for the industries we have studied so far. An additional reason for this decision was that firms are usually unwilling to provide information in sufficient detail for it to be possible to make valid comparisons, and we should have had to rely on published information. For other industries the variation in the products produced by plants may be less marked, and data on costs from a number of firms readily available. In these circumstances it might be possible to make use of cost data to measure the economies of scale though many qualifications would relate to comparisons of such costs. The main published sources of data on revenue and costs are the accounts of public companies and censuses of production. We discuss below the particular drawbacks of these sources because other economists have used them to draw conclusions about economies of scale.

The accounts of public companies. Most public companies are multi-plant firms and many operate in more than one industry simultaneously. Thus apart from the difficulties of measuring scale and costs there is a problem of comparability, and for the industries studied this alone rules out the use of accounts as a way of determining the economies of scale. Oil companies operate in different parts of the world and the extent to which they are vertically integrated varies. Steel and footwear companies specialise in different types of product and some of the latter own retail outlets. For book-printing there is the additional difficulty that there are very few public companies in the industry.

Companies are not required by law to publish details of their turnover or their total payroll, and so the only measure of size available for many companies is the capital employed. The value of capital employed by a company can be valued either by using balance sheet values, which are usually in terms of historical costs, or by using the stock exchange valuation. The changing level of prices makes the former method of valuation unsatisfactory, and the volatile performance of share prices and the fact that they discount differences in efficiency, including those attributable to variations in scale, invalidates any conclusions based on their use. In any case, capital employed is only a partial measure of scale.

<u>Census of production data</u>. The only measure of size for which the U.K. census data is analysed is the number of employees per establishment and, in the latest full census, employees per enterprise. The censuses show gross output and net output per employee and other data relating to employees. Professor Johnston(1) has drawn attention to the bias that this classification may introduce. An illustration of this bias is provided by considering two plants which have the same output but differing efficiency, as measured by output per employee. The most efficient plant will tend to be included in a lower-size group, and this bias may camouflage any economies of scale. Also, small establishments as measured by output may tend to make use of relatively labour intensive methods of production but as the census gives no measure of capital input it is not possible to gauge to what extent, if any, additional revenue or value added per employee in large establishments is a reflection of higher capital costs per employee. In addition, the quality of labour used may be linked to size, so that numbers employed may not even be an adequate measure of labour input.

Another drawback of census data is that establishments which are not strictly comparable are grouped together for census purposes. The problems of classification are caused partly by plants which make more than one type of product (for example an oil refinery which also makes petro-chemicals), partly by the grouping together in one industry of plants making non-competing products (for example Rolls Royce and Ford cars), and partly by the inclusion of plants with differing degrees of vertical integration (for example some shoe factories buy out soles already cut to size and some make their own). In addition, if census data is used, plants constructed at different times and using different techniques and factors of production cannot be distinguished from one another.

Another possible method of measuring the relationship between production costs and scale of output is to compare the costs of production and output over time for an individual plant which has expanded. Again there are problems involved in measuring the output of plants not making a homogeneous product over time, and in eliminating changes in costs not directly related to changes in scale of production. Another basic problem is that there is no accurate method of distinguishing between reductions in unit costs caused by increasing scale and those caused by improvements in methods independent of scale.

In addition many plants are not flexible as regards scale unless flexibility is deliberately provided for when a plant is first built. For example, if additional land is not acquired when a factory is built its expansion may be impossible. If this sort of flexibility is provided for in the original plant it will have increased the cost of constructing the plant. If it has not been provided for, the cost of extending the plant, plus the original cost of construction, may well exceed the cost of constructing an entirely new plant. It may conceivably be possible to estimate the economies of scale by this method, by making approximate adjustments for the effect

---

(1) J. Johnston, <u>Statistical Cost Functions</u>. New York 1960.

of technical progress and for indivisibilities of capital expenditure, but this has not been done in these studies except insofar as businessmen have used their experience of expanding plants when providing us with estimates of the economies of scale.

2. The structure of industries

The use of the changing structure of an industry to estimate the optimum level of capacity for the plants in an industry has been discussed by C. J. Stigler(1) and T. R. Saving.(2) Saving has suggested that

> there is a rather simple and straight-forward method available for the estimation of optimum size, whether it be plants or firms which are involved. This method is based on the economic definition that those sizes of plants which have minimum costs will be the sizes of plants which will survive the best in the market place. Hence if we simply find that a certain size of plant is gaining more and more of the total industry output, we can say with almost complete certainty that this size of plant lies within the range of optimum size of plants.

Even if this method could provide us with an estimate of the optimum size of plants and firms, and hence give an indication of the existence of economies of scale, it will not tell us the shape of the long-run average cost curve or give us any indication of the forces determining the optimum size. Also, there are qualifications to the reliability with which the changing structure of an industry can indicate the optimum size of plants or firms. In many industries there are elements of oligopoly, and the existence of goodwill can also be a potent force maintaining inefficient producers. In one industry we studied, large-scale producers acknowledged that some of the small-scale producers operating in one section of the industry were inefficient. But the large-scale producers refrained from directly competing with them because of long standing connexions. In some industries the total market is too small, and/or growing too slowly, for firms in competition to build large plants of optimum technical scale, because this would involve either heavy losses, while other firms with smaller plants were squeezed out, or the operation of plant at less than full capacity for a considerable period. Firms in these circumstances may build plants of 'sub-optimal' scale.

The method of using the changing structure of an industry to indicate the optimum size of plants owes something to biological theories about the survival of the fittest, which may have little relevance for plants (or firms) in a continuously fully employed economy. In such an economy the forces tending to squeeze out inefficient producers are weak, although take-over bids may operate to eliminate high-cost plants. There is no guarantee that they will do so, however. They may even be a means of prolonging their existence. For all these reasons, the changing structure of an industry may reflect only very imperfectly the optimum scale in terms of production costs.

---

(1) C. J. Stigler, 'Economies of Scale', in J. Law Economics 1958

(2) T. R. Saving, 'Estimation of Optimum Size of Plant by the Survivor Technique, in Quart. J. Economics. Nov. 1961.

2 Book Printing

Introduction

We had at first intended to make a study of the economies of scale for both book publishing and book printing. In many cases, however, the two functions are carried out by different firms, and publishing houses are often small-scale enterprises whose work does not involve 'techniques of production' in the usual sense of the phrase. In the event we decided to concentrate on book printing.(1)

The Census of Production 1958 records that there were in that year 61 enterprises, or firms, with 25 or more employees, whose main product was printed books. An analysis by size of these firms is shown in table 2.1. The table shows that three-quarters of the labour force of these firms was employed by firms with less than 1,000 employees and that the industry is organised in relatively small-scale units.(2)

Table 2.1. The Structure of the Book-printing Industry in 1958

Number of Employees	Number of Enterprises	Total Sales £th.	Total Employment
25-99	19	1,455	1,154
100-499	28	8,804	6,519
500-999	11	9,867	8,138
1,000 & over	3	9,217	5,413
	61	29,343	21,225

Source: Data supplied by the Board of Trade from the Census of
Production 1958.

---

(1) Most of the information on which this chapter is based was collected during 1961 and 1962.

(2) For manufacturing industries as a whole 45% of the labour force was employed in 1958 by enterprises with less than 1,000 employees. If enterprises with less than 25 employees are excluded 41% were employed by such firms.

In addition to the 60 or so specialist book-printing houses shown in the table, there are general printers who undertake book-printing work. In 1958 books to a value of £16.8 m. were printed and published by 149 enterprises, and to a value of £18.6 m. were printed for other U.K. publishers by 227 enterprises.(1) These figures illustrate the fragmented character of the industry.

With the exception of repeat printing orders and new editions of old titles, printers make a succession of new products, and in many cases a printer has in effect a temporary monopoly in the printing of those books he prints. Also the size, shape, type of print, number and type of illustrations and formulae also vary from book to book and because of this variation it is not possible to measure the scale of a printing house or the industry just in terms of the number of books printed. We have had to consider the implications for unit costs of:

1. The number of copies of an edition printed and the size of individual printing orders for a title.

2. Repeat printing orders for an edition and new editions of a title.

3. The degree of physical standardisation of titles printed.

4. The number of titles printed.

For readers who are not familiar with the technical processes employed in the industry we outline these in the Appendix to this chapter. Before describing our estimates of the relationships between scale and unit costs, we give a breakdown of the costs of book printing in the section that follows. In addition to the parts of the chapter devoted to the relationships listed above, we describe some cost comparisons for printing presses with varying levels of capacity in the fourth section. In the final sections of the chapter we describe the economies of paperback book printing, outline the impact of recent technical developments in the industry, and discuss the relationship between managerial and financial factors and scale.

The Costs of Book Printing

The main differences between the costs of a book printer and the total costs of producing a book are that the publisher's costs, the author's remuneration, and usually the cost of paper and process blocks, are not included in the former. Printing paper is normally bought by the publisher and supplied to the printer, who stores it on the publisher's behalf until it is used. The cost of paper varies widely, depending on its quality, and the cost per copy for a title of average novel length and size can range from 6d. to more than 1s.

---

(1) These figures exclude the output of enterprises with less than 25 employees. The Census does not reveal the extent of double counting of enterprises in these two estimates.

The diversity of the products of the industry makes it difficult to generalise about the costs of book printing. The type of books printed, the average length of printing orders, the proportion of reprint orders, and the proportion of paper bought by the printer will affect the balance of the various types of costs. So with the proviso that they are understood to be the actual costs of one printer and not necessarily representative, we give below in table 2.2 a breakdown of the costs of a medium-sized book-printing house with 400 employees.

Table 2.2. Structure of Costs for a medium-sized Printing House in 1961 (1)

Composition Costs		As % of total costs	
Readers		7	
Drawing		2	
Keyboards		6	
Casting machines		6	
Compositors		23	
Foundry		3	
Plateroom		1	
Preparation of blocks		1	49
Printing Department Costs			
Machines:			
Make-Ready	11		
Run-on	14	25	
Bindery		16	
Stores		10	51
			100

Book-printing costs can be divided into two main categories, composition and printing department costs as follows:-

1. Composition costs comprise the sub-editorial or reading costs, the costs of any drawings and block-making necessary for illustrations, maps, graphs, etc., and the costs of keyboarding, casting, setting, imposing and correcting the type.

These processes involve a good deal of hand work. Where machines are involved, as in keyboarding and casting, the machines are of one standard

---

(1) The cost of paper is excluded.

size only, and even the smallest printer requires several, so that in general, though the possibility of shift working provides some flexibility, increases in output require duplication of these machines and therefore give no saving in average unit capital or operating costs. There are also specialised equipment and skills which are sometimes required in the composing department for some types of work.

2. Printing Department costs consist of the costs of operating printing presses, the folding of sheets and binding of books. They include, as well as costs which vary with the size of printing orders, an element of 'fixed' costs, because the printing presses,and to a lesser extent the folding and binding machines, need to be prepared, or 'made-ready', before they are used. The costs of operating the presses once they are made-ready are referred to as the run-on costs.

The make-ready cost is quite substantial in the case of flat-bed printing machines, on which dimensional adjustments have to be made at the beginning of the printing operations on account of the size of the sheet, the number and size of the pages per sheet, and the thickness and quality of paper, all of which can and do vary from book to book. In addition, adjustments have to be made, in order to compensate for minute vari- ations in the level of the cylinders and the height of the type metal, which show up as irregularities on the printed sheet—some letters printing too heavily, others too lightly.

Besides printing the sheets, a printer may fold them and bind the books, but the folding and binding are usually arranged by the publisher, not necessarily with the firm which does the printing, and there are many firms which bind only. The costs of making up the book, which vary widely according to quality, are important and include the costs of cutting the board and cloth, assembling the cover, cutting the pages to size, and attaching the cover.

The Economies of Large Printing Orders

A high proportion of total printing costs are fixed in relation to the out- put of an edition of a title and the size of printing orders. To illustrate these relationships we have estimated the costs of printing a new title of 256 pages of a common size - crown octavo - with no illustrations or special composing problems. The 'fixed' costs assumed are: composition costs £275 and make-ready costs £75. The variable costs assumed are £10 per 1,000 copies for run-on costs, £30 per 1,000 copies for paper and £30 per 1,000 copies for binding. The unit run-on costs are usually constant whatever the number of copies of a title printed, except for the first 1,000 or so sheets, which generally take a little longer to print because it takes some time for the machines to be got up to their normal speed of impression and to produce the required quality. The size of printing orders also has a small effect on other unit variable costs but the relative stability of these costs does exert a damping effect on the economies of large printing orders.

Book-printing costs per copy for initial printing orders of various sizes based on these assumptions are shown in table 2.3. To put the number of copies printed into perspective, a normal first printing order for a 'run of the mill' novel might be about 10,000 copies. This table clearly illustrates the economies which can be achieved by spreading composition and make-ready costs.

Table 2.3. Printing Costs for a 256-page Book (for initial printing orders of varying size)

Number of copies printed	Cost per copy excluding the cost of paper and binding	Cost per copy including the cost of paper and binding
	s. d	s d
1,000	7 2	8 5
5,000	1 7	2 10
10,000	11	2 1
20,000	7	1 9
50,000	4	1 6

Many of the economies of large printing orders are also obtained by repeat orders. Compared with a new title, the printing costs for a reprint order exclude a major part of the original composition costs but the reduction in composition costs might be partly offset by higher make-ready costs if the type has become very worn. Composition costs for a reprint order of the title described above would be about £12 if the type had been stored in chase ready for printing and £32 if it had been taken out of chase and stored separately. This compares with our estimate for composition costs for the new title of £275.

Assuming that the composition costs for a reprint order are £32 and that the make-ready costs are £75—i.e. there is no increase in the make-ready costs because of worn type—then the additional composition and make-ready costs for two printing orders of the book already considered in this section, compared to one, would be £107. Spread over 2,000 copies this amounts to 1s. per copy but spread over 20,000 copies to only 1d. per copy. The choice facing publishers can be illustrated by comparing the cost of printing 10,000 copies of the title described above in one or two printing orders. In making this comparison the cost of paper has been included, but the cost of binding has been excluded because printed sheets rather than bound books are usually stored. The cost of printing 10,000 copies as one order would be £750 and the marginal cost of the last five thousand would be £200. The cost for an initial order of 5,000 copies would be £550 and a second printing order for 5,000 copies would cost £307. If less than 5,000 copies are sold in all, the saving by printing an initial order of 5,000 rather than 10,000 would be £200. On the other hand, if more than 5,000 copies can be sold, and a second printing order has to be made, the loss by not having an initial printing order of 10,000 copies would be £107, if the second printing order is for 5,000 copies. A cost which has to be set against any savings achieved by large printing orders is the cost of storing sheets.

It is impossible to generalise about the costs of new editions of old titles because the extent to which type, layout etc. are altered varies. Economies will only occur if old type can be used.

The Economies of Large Machines

From looking at the process of printing a book we should expect that if technical economies of scale exist in this industry one place where they would appear is in the machine room and bindery. It is only in these departments, where printing, folding and binding machines are used, that there are likely to be found the possibilities of savings associated with large indivisible items of capital equipment. We have estimated the cost of operating printing presses and folding machines of varying capacity to see how important these economies are.

The most common type of printing press used in letterpress book printing is the flat-bed machine, which works on the principle of the formes of type being laid in the bed of the machine, which passes in a reciprocating motion, first under inking rollers and then under impression rollers over which the sheets of paper are fed. These machines may be either single-sided, which print on one side of the sheet at each impression, so that the sheets have to be turned over and fed in again later for the other side to be printed, or 'perfector' machines, which print on both sides of the sheet at the same pass through the machine.

Rotary letterpress machines are a fairly recent introduction into book printing, although the rotary press was invented in 1848,(1) and has been used in newspaper printing for many years. The main reasons for its absence in the book printing house seems to have been the belief that the necessary high quality of impression could not be achieved from the curved plates which are used in a rotary press and the extra cost of making plates for short-run non-repeating titles if printed on a rotary press. The distinctive feature of the rotary press is of course the high speed of impression which it can achieve compared to a flat-bed machine, the speed of which is limited by the reciprocating action of the bed.

Although newspapers are printed on rotary presses at speeds in excess of 40, 000 sheets per hour, the quality of impression demanded is much lower than for books, and 6-10, 000 sheets per hour seems to be the maximum order of speed that rotary machines can achieve in book printing. But the typical speed of a flat-bed letterpress is 1, 200-1, 500 sheets per hour.

To determine the relative costs of printing books on different sizes and types of machine, comparative cost studies were made of printing a given 'standard' book. Only the costs which were directly attributable to using the particular presses and folding machines were considered, and those

---

(1) S. H. Steinberg, Five Hundred Years of Printing, Penguin Books, 1955.

overhead charges which would not be affected by the size and type of machine used were ignored. The costs included in our analyses were the depreciation charges for presses and folding machines, the wages of machine operators, and electric power and maintenance costs.

Printing and folding machines are known by the maximum size of the sheet they will print, described either in inches or by traditional printing expressions. Thus a machine which will print a sheet 40" × 30" is known as a Quad-Crown machine, and each side of a sheet will have room for 32 crown-octavo pages. An 8-Crown machine prints a sheet of 40" × 60", on which 64 pages of a crown-octavo book can be printed.

We assumed for our calculations that the size of the page of the book determined which size of machine was suitable for the job. For example, a crown-octavo book could be printed on either a Quad-Crown or 8-Crown machine. In practice, there are reasons which prevent fully efficient machine loading. Printers often use a machine which is 'unsuitable' in the above sense, and thereby fail to utilise the maximum available printing area of the presses. But apart from the few pages at the end of the book which do not make up into a multiple of 32 pages, and such extras as illustrations and tables, books are rarely printed on presses of less than Quad size. The cost comparisons were therefore confined to machines of Quad and 8 size, the latter being the largest used.

1. Flat-Bed Machines

To make comparisons we divided printing press costs into three main categories—depreciation, make-ready and run-on costs. The larger flat-bed machines were individually more expensive, and so the depreciation charge—estimated on the basis of replacement cost—was higher per machine, but on the basis of depreciation per book printed the charge was lower, provided that the larger machines were operated at a high level of capacity. The make-ready time was not greatly affected by the size of the machine used, because the cost was determined by the total area of type to be printed, which was of course assumed to be the same in each case. Though the speed of the bigger machines, in terms of the number of impressions per hour, is little different from that for smaller machines, they print a greater area of type at each impression, and incur labour costs only marginally greater than for smaller machines. Thus the run-on cost per book printed was lower for the bigger machines.

In order to be cheaper, larger machines need to have a certain minimum amount of 'running time'. The running time is determined by the number of titles printed and the number of copies of each title. The greater the average number of copies of each title the greater the advantage of larger presses. Thus the economies of large machines are an added prize for large printing orders.

Almost without exception our comparisons of machine costs showed it to be cheaper to print on a larger machine above a certain output as measured by the size of printing order and the number of titles printed. We have illustrated the economies of large machines by calculating the costs of printing 5,000 copies of 450 titles of a standard size on two machines, a Quad-Crown and an 8-Crown perfector. The estimated costs per title are set out in table 2.4. In this case the costs for the larger machine are 31 per cent lower than for the smaller machine, assuming both are used to full capacity. These costs represent about 25 per cent of the costs of book printing, excluding the cost of paper, so the econo- mies of the larger machines represent about 8 per cent of the total costs of book printing. For printing orders of less than 5,000 copies the economies would be smaller.

Table 2.4. Comparative Printing Press and Folding Costs for two Flat-bed Printing Presses. — 5,000 copies of a standard title.

	Quad-Crown Single sided	8-Crown Perfector
Cost per title for machines operating at full capacity.	£	£
—Depreciation (1)	26	20
—Make-ready	24	24
—Run-on	36	15
	86	59

2. Rotary Machines

At the time this research was undertaken there were relatively few rotary machines in use for book work, and our conclusions about their costs are therefore tentative. A rotary letterpress machine prints on either a sheet or a continuous roll or web of paper, and a continuous folding attachment can be added at the delivery end of the press. Both web-feeding and continuous folding greatly speed up the rate of produc- tion.

In spite of the higher capital cost of rotary machines, depreciation per sheet printed is lower than for flat-bed machines provided a certain level of output is achieved, because the speed of impression on rotary presses is so much higher. For printing with a flat-bed press it is possible to print with the type but for printing on a rotary press it is necessary to make printing plates. However the time needed to make a rotary machine ready for printing is much lower than for a flat bed, because the cylin- ders are more precisely engineered than flat-bed cylinders, and because the methods of manufacturing and preparing the printing plates are far more effective in producing a plane surface of the correct height than the methods of producing the metal type, or electro or stereo plates for flat-bed machines.

---

(1) 10 per cent of the estimated replacement value.

Above a certain level of output, the cost advantages of lower make-ready times and much faster running speeds outweigh the higher depreciation charge per machine and the additional cost of making plates. To illustrate these economies we estimated costs for printing 5, 000 copies of 450 titles of a standard size with a rotary press with attached folders, instead of with an 8-Crown perfector flat-bed machine with separate folding machines. Our estimate suggested that the costs per title with the rotary press would be 27 per cent less than with the flat-bed machine.

At this point it may be as well to emphasise the assumptions on which these calculations have been based, for they are in no sense a sufficient reason for jumping to conclusions and recommending wholesale re-organisation of book-printing houses. First full capacity working is assumed. Second it is assumed that all books are 256 pages long, with the same size of pages, with the same size area of type and the same problems of making-ready on the machine. Third, 5, 000 copies of each title are assumed to be printed. In practice of course this standardisation does not exist and some printing orders are for a small number of copies so that the full advantages of the faster running speeds of larger presses cannot be reaped. Small machines are required to print small orders and odd short runs. These smaller machines are also used for dust jackets, particularly if they are capable of printing with coloured ink.

The Economies of Standardisation

The great variety of work that a book printer is called upon to do in printing books has already been mentioned. Apart from variations in the size of books and their content there is variety in type faces. This occurs in the size of the face, its character, and the body of the type. The variety of type means that a very large stock of metal must be kept if type itself is stored, and even if matrices only of the type are kept a lot of capital is tied up in this way. There are also differences in the sizes of pages and margins, and a sufficient stock of metal framework must be kept to cover all the sizes which might be required. The following quotations from a report of a Printing and Allied Trades Research Association research team shows the extent of the variations. (1) 'One firm, for example, has 27 different book page sizes within the range 5" × 7" to $5\frac{1}{2}$" × 8".... some sizes vary from one another by only a sixteenth of an inch in one direction. This same firm has in current production one hundred and sixteen different page sizes, almost half of this number falling between $4\frac{1}{2}$" × $6\frac{1}{2}$" and $6\frac{1}{2}$" × $8\frac{1}{2}$". This is a fair-sized firm with 89 compositors.'

This multiplicity of sizes results also in many adjustments having to be made to printing, folding and binding machinery and equipment. This is not only expensive because of the labour and the loss of machine-time involved. The equipment has to be capable of being adjusted, and this causes it to be more expensive particularly if, as often happens, the

---

(1) D.S.I.R., Productivity in Letterpress Printing, H.M.S.O., 1961.

range of adjustment on a machine is determined by an individual printer's requirements and the machine has therefore to be custom-built.

It appears then that considerable economies of standarisation are available to the book printer, particularly for a small-scale printer, if he is prepared to limit the almost infinite variety of page sizes, type faces and sizes, and other facilities which he normally offers to publishers. One reason why small-scale printers fail to specialise is that they fear that if they refuse to print other works they will not be offered the chance of printing the type of books in which they primarily specialise.

The Effects on Costs of Printing more Titles

Since the output of any one title is limited by the demand for that title, printers can only achieve a larger output by printing a larger number of titles. We have seen that there are economies to be obtained by using large printing presses and by specialisation. A printer printing 250 titles (1) a year can fully employ a high speed rotary press but for some types of work, e.g. for short runs, a smaller press has lower unit costs. In practice printers usually accept a variety of work which cannot be performed on one type of press, and many printers have presses idle from time to time. In practice securing the full utilisation of press capacity is a problem for both small and large-scale printing houses.

It is possible for a printer operating on a small scale to be competitive if he limits the range of work he accepts. For most types of book printing a medium-size printing house with 300-400 employees could certainly achieve all the technical economies of scale available if it did specialise. Clearly any such estimate must be very approximate, and must depend on the type of work undertaken. Book printers with less than 300-400 employees can for certain types of work be fully competitive. We visited one printer, with a staff of only 40, who by specialising in printing a limited range of books with printing runs of from five to thirty thousand, by using up to-date processes e.g. lino-type machines, and by keeping management overheads to a minimum was able to quote very competitive prices. As a guide to the relationship between the size of a printing house in relation to that of the whole industry, a printer with a labour force of 300-400 would employ less than 2 per cent of the total labour force of the firms whose main product is printed books. He would of course employ an even smaller proportion of the total labour force employed in printing books if a proportion of the labour force of general printers who undertake book printing work is included.

---

(1) It is assumed that each title is of a standard size and that 5,000 copies of each are printed.

Paperbacks

Sir Allen Lane began his risky paperback publishing venture in 1935. He aimed to reach a new public, which he believed existed, which would want to buy good-quality books, at first fiction and then later non-fiction, at low prices. He could provide the low prices, 6d. per copy, only if print orders were big enough to get sufficient economies of long runs. The first ten titles had a print order of 20, 000 copies each. From the earlier discussion of the economies of scale resulting from larger editions and from using rotary machines, we can appreciate how the printing of paperback books can achieve economies, often to a significant degree.

First, paperbacks of the Penguin type are typically books with a large appeal, often proven by the success of earlier publications in hard cover form. This means long runs and the economies which result. Secondly, the fixed costs of making-ready the printing and folding machines are reduced if these machines are used for several paperback titles; the machines do not require dimensional adjustment because paperbacks tend to be of the same size. Thirdly, the large editions, standardised format, and often standardised type of paper mean that the printing of paperbacks is very suitable for a web-fed, rotary machine with attached continuous-folder. Quality of impression is not considered quite so important in paperbacks as in hard cover books, and there is no objection to using flexible, rubber or plastic printing plates on the rotary machine.

Large rotary machines, of the type used for producing paperbacks, show a cost advantage over smaller rotary machines. This is most marked if the larger machines have a continuous folding attachment and the smaller have not, as is quite common. We have compared the cost of printing 25, 000 copies per title on two types of rotary press, a Rotary Press R with an 8-Crown Folder which has a capacity of about 50 titles a year and a Web-fed Rotary Press with a folding attachment having a capacity of about 115 titles a year.(1) The saving in printing press and folding costs for the larger rotary press represent 42 per cent of the costs for the smaller press, assuming both presses are used to full capacity.

We have obtained estimates of the relationship between printing costs and the number of copies printed for paperbacks. These are based on the quotations of printers. The estimates are shown in table 2.5 and demonstrate the immense economies of large printing orders for paperbacks. These economies continue up to high levels of output and, because of the low cost of the paper used and the absence of case binding, these economies are not so damped down as for case-bound books. The cost of printing and paper falls from 1s. 9d. per copy for printing orders of 5, 000 copies to 6d. per copy for orders of 200, 000.

The additional costs of a repeat printing order would include the setting and making of moulds and plates etc. for the pages and cover. The estimated effect of printing two orders of 50, 000 copies each compared to

---

(1) It is assumed that each title has 256 pages and that 25, 000 copies of each title are printed.

one order for 100,000 copies is that printing costs per thousand copies are increased by £2. For smaller reprint orders the difference would be proportionately larger.

Cost advantages of the sort achieved for paperbacks of the 'Penguin' type do not apply in full to the printing of 'Quality' paperbacks. These are often students' editions of books which do not appeal to a large number of readers and cannot gain as many of the economies of long runs as a traditional paperback. They can be sold at lower prices than hardcover editions partly because the cost of binding is greatly reduced, partly because it may be possible to make use of the type set up for hardback printing, and thus save a substantial proportion of the composition costs, and partly because the author's royalty may be reduced. In addition—and very important—a paperback printing order will be larger than for a hard-back.

Table 2.5. Printing Costs for Paperbacks in 1961

Printing Order Number	Printing Costs per 1,000 copies	Paper Cost per 1,000 copies (1)	Total	Index of total cost (cost per copy for 5,000 copies = 100)
	£	£	£	
5,000	72	14	86	100
10,000	56	13	69	80
20,000	38	13	51	59
50,000	22	13	35	41
100,000	16	13	29	34
200,000	13	13	26	30

Future developments

1. Photo composition

The high costs of composition are due primarily to the large amount of handwork involved. These high fixed costs can be reduced as a proportion of average unit costs by increasing the number of copies printed, but the market sets a limit to this. There is, therefore, a strong incentive to reduce average costs by reducing the costs of composition, and a method of composition which reduces the amount of handwork is initially attractive as a means of doing this. Photo composition is such a method, and although there are several systems at present being developed, the principle of each is the same. The operation of a key-board causes a film to be exposed with the selected character in the selected type face. This film is then photographed on to a sensitised plate, during which operation the size of the characters can usually be determined within a wide range. This plate can then be used on an offset lithopress (see below), or to make a duplicate plate for use on a printing press. Thus metal type is completely eliminated from the composition process, and such problems as corrections are tackled by machine rather than by hand.

As could be expected, the equipment for this is expensive, especially since it is mostly in the prototype stage. The degree of automation varies from one system to another and is reflected in the price range which is about £30,000 to £100,000. Nevertheless it shows sufficient promise for some printers to be prepared to try one of the systems for book printing. Another eventual possibility is the use of computers for composition to reduce the amount of handwork involved.

2. Offset lithography

This is a method of printing by which the image is offset from the printing plate on to a roller and thence on to the paper. Offset lithography is a very suitable way of reprinting a book, particulary if the type is very worn or has been destroyed and if no moulds have been taken. The impression produced by the offset process is 'softer' than that of letter-press, but it provides better illustrations than the half-tone blocks used in the letterpress method. Offset lithography printing presses are almost all rotary machines, and therefore have the advantage of high speed. Also make-ready times for such machines are shorter. Offset lithography is being increasingly used in reprint book work.

In the future the combination of photo composition with either rotary letterpress or offset lithography seems likely to be used for an increasing amount of book printing. If this forecast is correct, the effect on the possibilities for economies of scale are likely to be significant. First, photo composition will offer the possibilities of lower costs of composition, provided the output of the printing house is large enough to justify the capital cost which is at present about £100,000. Second, offset lithography or rotary letterpress both offer their significant savings if they can be combined with highly mechanised and automated binding departments. This qualification implies either the high output associated with long runs of paperback books, since these are of a standardised format which is suitable for such equipment as continuous folding attachments, or it implies a much greater standardisation of page and book sizes.

Managerial and Financial Factors and Scale

The effects of scale of output on managerial and administrative costs are notoriously difficult to measure, and we have not been able to obtain data which throw light on them. All we have are impressionistic ideas obtained from our visits to printing firms.

In the firms employing less than about 800 workers, the managing director was convinced of the value of his personal knowledge and control in the day-to-day management of his firm, and considered his present size to be pretty close to the optimum for managerial efficiency. Each manager thought that the problems of co-ordination and lack of personal contact involved in expansion much beyond his present size would lead to a reduction in efficiency and to a rise in average costs. In the larger firms there was not this emphasis on the virtues of personal control nor, understandably enough perhaps, on the dangers of lack of proper co-ordination resulting from expansion beyond a certain size of enterprise.

Our impression was that the ability of the managing director is important and that some operated best in a small environment and others were more suited to a larger firm. A high standard of management enabled one very small firm, for example, to compete with much bigger firms, which it would otherwise not have been able to do, since it lacked a separate sales organisation, had no specialist administrative services and a very small financial base to cushion it against any substantial trading fluctuations.

Financial considerations in book printing are important. Machinery is expensive, although long-lasting, and capital requirements of a firm starting from scratch and employing a total staff of about 500 would be approximately £ 750, 000. In 1961 new rotary letterpress machines cost from £ 12, 000 to £ 32, 000 each, and the scanty data on capital expenditure given in the Board of Trade's Census of Production Report for 1958 do not suggest that the general level of expenditure on new capital equipment allows such machines to be bought very often. A purely personal and amateur estimate of the number of rotary letterpress machines used in this country for bookwork in 1961 is 20. The reasons for this scarcity of machines which are faster and cheaper to run than flat-bed machines are many, but among them is certainly availability of capital. The need for capital is not confined to the machine room either, for much of the value of fast-running rotary machines is lost if equally fast-running folding attachments and automated binding equipment is not combined with them.

Conclusions

Our study of economies of scale in the book-printing industry has illustrated some of the different dimensions of scale for which economies may apply. The most obvious economies of scale in book printing are associated with increasing the size of printing orders. These economies result mainly from the spreading of composition and make-ready costs. In addition there are economies which can be achieved by the use of high-capacity presses and folding machines, the full benefit of which can only be obtained when printing large orders. There are also economies of standardisation and specialisation and finally there are economies which a printer can achieve by expanding his total output. But a printer can only print more books by printing more titles - he cannot decide to print more copies of the same number of titles - this decision is the publisher's and is based on the public's demand for particular books.

What is the significance of these economies of scale for individual book-printers? It is clear that maximum economies of scale can only be obtained when all five types of economies are available at the same time. This is possible for paperback book printing and it seems likely that there will continue to be a trend for a higher proportion of the total output of the industry to come from large-scale paperback book printers. Nevertheless, specialist printers will continue to be able to earn a comparable rate of profit per unit of capital employed because of the price which their product commands. Book printers employing a small proportion of the industry's labour force, less than 2 per cent, can be competitive. Though the size of the labour force is only an approximate guide to the output of a printer in terms of the value of sales, it is clear that a printer with a small share of the total book printing market can achieve all the significant economies of scale in this industry.

At the present time many small-scale printers do not achieve the full benefits of standardisation and specialisation and there is scope in the industry for further improvements in this direction.

For the industry as a whole economies of scale are also significant. In the past the number of copies of hard-back titles bought has been limited partly because of the ability of the public to borrow books at negligible cost from libraries. The demand for paperbacks, at a fraction of the price of hard-backs, is much greater, and for reprints of novels may be of the order of 20, 000 copies compared with about 2, 000 for a hard-back. The trend towards printing more paperbacks, and in some cases printing the paperback edition first, is operating to increase the average number of copies of each title printed. The continuing improvement in the standard of education together with increased incomes can be expected to operate in the same direction. It is therefore plausible to assume that a part of the future increase in output of the industry will take the form of an increase in the number of copies of each title printed. On the basis of our estimates of the economies of scale, we should expect this growth to be associated with substantial savings in costs.

Appendix to Chapter 2

A Layman's Guide to the Processes used in Book Printing

This is a layman's guide with no pretence to comprehensiveness and refers to a typical book without illustrations.

1. The manuscript arrives at the printing house from the publisher, with instructions such as type face and size, size of pages, width of margins, type of binding, type of paper (which is supplied by the publisher and may well have been sent to the printer and kept by him in his 'white store' some weeks in advance of the printing order), and number of copies required.

2. The manuscript is read, to put it into house style (printer's and publisher's) which is done in order to regularise the use of alternative spellings such as -ise or -ize, the use of capitals and other similar points. At the same time a check on punctuation and spelling is made.

3. The manuscript is then put into type, and almost always, unless there is some peculiar problem of composition which necessitates composing by hand, one of two sorts of composing machine will be used. Both sorts are operated by a keyboard. The Monotype machine produces a punched paper tape which is used to control the operation of a separate casting machine, which produces, from a supply of hot metal, lead alloy characters in the order in which they have been 'typed' on the keyboard. The other sort of machine, made either by the Linotype or the Intertype company, selects a matrix of each character as the relevant key is struck by the operator and at the end of a line, which is automatically justified (spaced), the collection of matrices passes to another part of the machine where a supply of hot metal is kept and a line or 'slug' of type is cast and dropped down into the frame of the galley. The matrices then return to the store of matrices in the machine to be available for re-use.

4. The lines of type are cast into galleys, and galley proofs (proofs of two or three pages one above another on the same sheet of paper) are printed.

5. The galley proofs are read and corrected by printing house reader.

6. The proofs are sent to the author for correction.

7. The galleys of type are corrected to incorporate the author's alterations.

8. The type is imposed by hand into pages.

9. If reprints are expected or even thought likely, papier maché, wax or plastic moulds of the type are taken, and metal (rigid) or rubber or plastic (flexible) plates of one to four pages per plate made from them. This is done because after a certain length of run the type begins to wear and the quality of the printing deteriorates. These duplicate plates last for longer lengths of run than type and in any case can be replaced relatively cheaply by a new impression from the mould. Moreover the cost of storing them and the moulds is much less than storing the bulkier and more vulnerable type, and less money is tied up in the actual metal involved.

10. The pages of type are made up into 'formes' or the plates are made up on to 'beds'. That is, they are put down side by side and held rigid by metal clamps called 'chases', and are then placed on to the bed of the printing machine. The number of pages in the forme is determined by the size of the sheet which the machine will print. There is some variation in the sheet sizes which most flat-bed machines will take. The arrangement of the pages on the sheet is determined by the later operation of folding the sheet into a 'signature', which is the name given to the separate sections of a book. These can be distinguished by looking down on to the top or bottom edge of the spine of the book.

11. A proof is taken and read. It will also show unevenness in the impression, and thus the necessity for 'making-ready' the printing

machine. This process is one by which the machine minder 'builds up' in the necessary places the level of the printing cylinder, or the level of the forme, to eliminate variations in the intensity of impression, which cause some characters to be printed in a very heavy bold manner and may result in the clogging of small spaces, and others to be too faint. This 'patching' of the cylinder and under- and inter-laying of the forme may take many hours. In addition the position of the pages of type locked up within the forme, and the placing of the forme on the bed of the machine, must be checked and corrected to ensure proper registration and alignment of the printed pages when they are folded, cut, and made up into the book.

12. A proof is taken and used in the process of ensuring a proper ink flow in the machine.

13. The requisite number of sheets are 'run on', i.e. printed as they pass through the machine.

14. Sheets are passed through a folding machine, which folds each sheet into a section of the book called a 'signature'.

15. The sections are collated and then (probably) stitched.

16. The back of the book is rounded and a backing paper attached.

17. A separately made cover is attached.

3   The Footwear Industry

Introduction

There were 107,000 people employed by the 804 enterprises (or firms) in the footwear industry in 1958 and the industry's sales during that year were £170 m.(1) The 804 enterprises operated 1,025 establishments and an analysis by numbers employed for these establishments is shown in table 3.1. Some of the large number of small establishments make bespoke shoes or high-fashion or other speciality footwear.

Table 3.1. The size of establishments in the footwear industry

Average number of employees	Number of establishments %	Total sales £m	%	Total employment (000)	%
1-99	671	66	36	21	23	21
100-199	155	15	33	19	21	20
200-299	68	7	25	15	16	15
300-499	59	6	36	21	22	21
500-999	25	2	26	15	17	16
1000+	5	—	13	7	8	7
Unsatisfactory returns	42	4	1	—	1	—
	1,025	100	170	100	107	100

Source: Census of Production 1958

Many firms and most factories in the industry specialise in the production of a limited range of footwear and this specialisation may relate to men's, ladies' or children's shoes, to expensive, medium price or cheap shoes, to general purpose or casual shoes and to the methods of constructing shoes which are described below. Thus a factory may specialise in the production of cemented, medium-price women's shoes or cheap vulcanised men's shoes or hand made, ladies' fashion shoes.

---

(1) Census of Production 1958. The Census definition of the footwear trade includes the manufacture of footwear with fabric uppers and excludes rubber footwear.

Even with this specialisation, a range of styles, fittings, colours and of course sizes is usually made at each factory and for many the range of styles is continuously changing as fashions in footwear evolve. This diversity of output makes comparisons between factories and generalisations about the industry difficult.

One distinctive feature of the industry is the variation in the quality of the main raw material, leather. The quality of hides varies and there are variations in the properties of different parts of each hide. This, and the diversity of styles and sizes of shoes produced, has limited the scope for the introduction of automatic machinery, and most of the machines at present used are powered tools dependent for efficient operation on the skill of the operator.

We have divided our discussion of the economies of scale in the industry into six sections. In the next section, to provide a basis for a consideration of the economies of scale, we give a brief description of the processes and operations employed in the industry and the organisation of footwear factories, and we follow this in the third section with a breakdown of the costs of making shoes. In the fourth section we describe estimates of the economies of large factories, based on the artificial assumption that factories make one style of shoe, and in the fifth section we consider the effect on costs of dropping this assumption. In the last section we describe other evidence relating to economies of scale in the industry and give the conclusions of our study.

Before describing our estimates of the economies of scale we must mention some of the other forces which affect the viability of a shoe manufacturing business. This is necessary if the importance of economies of scale is to be seen in perspective. The quality of management is one of these forces. Up to two hundred separate operations may be involved in the manufacture of a pair of shoes, and many of these operations require skilled operatives. Good management in controlling production and achieving the best output by operatives is clearly important. Shoe manufacturing is a cyclical industry, being subject to seasonal and annual fluctuations in the level of trade, and a management which successfully maintains a steady flow of work may offset any disadvantages caused by operating on a small scale. A manufacturer may achieve a relatively even flow of work by owning retail outlets, and in practice some manufacturers own a chain of shops or hold sufficient shares in a retailing company to have some control over its buying policy. Other ways of achieving an even flow of work are sub-contracting during the boom phases of the cycle, or simply by keen salesmanship. Design is particularly important for women's shoes and is becoming much more important than hitherto for men's shoes. A flair for selecting successful styles, and foreseeing trends in design, is a decisive factor affecting the viability of some manufacturing units. Also the costs of capital vary between firms. Manufacturers who provide their own capital are sometimes willing to accept a small return on this capital, while firms operating with borrowed finance have to provide a higher rate of return. The success of a footwear manufacturing business thus depends on many factors of which the economies of scale is only one.

The processes used in manufacturing shoes and the organisation of footwear factories

The processes and operations employed in the manufacture of shoes vary between factories and within factories. This description is an outline of these processes and operations with no pretence to comprehensiveness.

Shoe factories are divided into departments or 'rooms' as they are called in the industry. In a modern shoe factory the main departments are the 'clicking' room in which the 'uppers' are cut, the 'closing' room, in which the parts of the upper are prepared and sewn together, the 'preparation' room in which the soles are cut and the heels prepared, the 'making' room in which the shoes are assembled, and the 'shoe' room in which shoes are inspected and made ready for despatch. In addition some manufacturers have a separate 'finishing' room where the shoe bottoms are trimmed, coloured and waxed.

In each department several operations are performed, the number depending on the type of shoe and the methods of production used. Table 3.2 gives a breakdown, by department and by type, of the operations used in making women's cemented court shoes. These estimates are based on the best practice in use in 1962.

Table 3.2. An analysis of the operations used in
manufacturing women's cemented court shoes

(a)	Operations by department		(b)	Operations by type	
	Clicking	10		Transport	6
	Closing	18		Hand	29
	Preparation	24		Machine	49
	Making	26		Automatic	4
	Shoe	12		Process (1)	2
		90			90

Source: Information obtained from the Shoe and Allied Trades Research Association.

The first step in making a shoe is to design it. Some manufacturers employ specialist designers, others prepare their own designs aided by trade papers or buy out designs at a cost of about £20 per style. From the designs a sample has to be made up and the operations to be used in production planned. Patterns for cutting upper parts have to be made and materials procured. Separate patterns are usually made for each size of shoe,(2) but a 'grading' machine is available for making various

---

(1) An example of a process operation is the heating of a shoe on a 'last' to make it rapidly take the shape of the last.

(2) In practice one pattern may be used for two or even more sizes and fittings but this may involve some trimming of the shoe.

sizes once a master pattern has been cut. Small firms can buy out these grading operations at a cost of about £30 per style.

The cutting of the 'uppers' of shoes or 'clicking' can be performed by hand, in which case the clicker uses a knife to cut around a brass rimmed, cardboard pattern, or by press, for which the clicker requires a press knife which he places on the leather, preparatory to press stamping the part. Clicking is a highly skilled trade because of the variation in the quality of leather, the need to match parts of the upper, and the need to economise leather. Press cutting is approximately fifty per cent faster than hand cutting, and a skilled clicker can cut uppers for approximately 125 pairs of women's court shoes a day by press. The rental of a press and the costs of running it are approximately £150 a year. A clicker's wages amounted to between £1,000 and £1,250 a year in the London area in 1963.

The cost of press knives depends on their quality, size and intricacy. A set of press knives for the parts for a range of sizes of women's court shoe may cost as little as £100 and knives costing this much would cut say 10,000 pairs each. Good quality dies, which will last indefinitely, cost considerably more. At least some new knives are usually required for each new style and the need to change styles limits the use of press cutting because of the cost of the knives. Another factor operating in the same direction is the payment of clickers by piece rates. These are lower per pair for press clicking than for hand clicking but do not fully discount the increased productivity which can be achieved by using a press. Where long runs of a style are achieved however the difference in costs for press and hand clicking is likely to be of the order of 3d. per pair.

Usually the work of each clicker is organised independently. He draws a supply of leather from the leather store and cuts parts from it. When the parts have been cut they are bundled together in batches and returned to the store or passed to the closing department. A clicker usually cuts all the outer parts for a shoe so that the parts match, and less experienced clickers cut the linings for the uppers. Alternatively, clickers may cut different parts for the uppers, particularly where the material used is plastic or a fabric which does not vary in quality or texture. At factories where long runs of each style, colour and size are made a clicker may work on one style of shoe indefinitely, and will draw large batches of leather at a time. At others, where fashion shoes are made, he may only make a few of each style at a time, particularly towards the end of a season.

A number of distinct operations are carried out in the closing room. These include marking the uppers with an identification number, 'skiving' the leather to reduce its thickness (this is required to avoid seams being unsightly and uncomfortable), perforating parts for decoration and stitching and cementing parts of the upper together. The machines used in the closing room are relatively inexpensive as compared with the labour costs involved.

The output of operatives on the different operations performed in a closing room varies considerably. F. G. Bailey and G. Denton calculated the output for 16 operations used in the closing rooms of 12 factories making men's shoes. The average output of the three most efficient factories for the 16 operations varied between 150 and 4, 500 pairs a day with a median output of 1, 025 pairs a day.(1) This variation in output for different operations involves a problem of balancing which is discussed in more detail below.

If shoes have to be perforated for purposes of decoration the operation can be carried out by press or by hand punching. Press stamping is very much quicker than the hand punching of holes, but the cost of press patterns which may amount to £50 is prohibitive unless long runs of a pattern are required.

One method of organising the work in a closing room is to use a conveyor belt to carry trays with batches of parts. The operatives, invariably women in this department, are seated with their equipment such as sewing or skiving machines on either side of the conveyor and the supervisor or assistant controls the despatch of trays to each operative independently. When an operation has been completed, the batch is returned on the conveyor and is sent to the appropriate operative for the next operation to be performed. Instead of using a conveyor belt, trays of work may be carried to the operatives. Alternatively, where long runs of each style of shoes are made, the work can be passed, on trolleys containing parts for hundreds of pairs of a single size of shoe, to each operative in turn.

The 'bottoms' or soles and heels of shoes are cut, prepared, and assembled in the preparation room, and the output of some of the presses used in this department can be of the order of 3, 000 or more pairs a day. Many firms buy out soles and heels already cut and shaped to size, and this practice has increased during recent years. The figure of 24 operations performed in the preparation room, shown in table 3.2, gives an exaggerated impression of the current importance of this department.

In the making room, the 'uppers' are first pulled over a 'last' and attached to the 'insole', and then the 'bottom' is attached to the 'upper' and 'insole'. A last is a wood or plastic model of a foot. The original methods of attaching the bottoms to the uppers of shoes were nailing and stitching. Table 3.3 shows the extent to which these methods have and are being superseded by the various methods of cementing and moulding. The Goodyear welted, machine sewn, and Veldschoen methods all involve attaching the sole by stitching, and the proportion of shoes made by these methods fell from 41 to 20 per cent of the shoes made in the British Isles between 1957 and 1962.

The table shows the increase in the use of cemented construction, and this trend, which has been aided by the development of improved quick-setting cementing compounds, is continuing. Cemented construction already predominates in the production of women's shoes, as it is particularly appropriate for shoes with thin soles, and is gaining ground in the production of men's shoes. Other relatively new methods of construction involve moulding a sole to the upper and insole. The vulca-

_____

(1) F. G. Bailey and G. Denton, 'A Productivity Survey of Twelve Closing Rooms (Men's Shoes)'. J. Boot Shoe Indus., April, 1953.

nising processes are methods whereby a rubber soling compound in a non-vulcanised condition is press cured to the upper and insole. In this country the use of this type of construction began in the 1950's and has grown very rapidly in recent years. Injection moulding of plastic soles is the latest development in methods of constructing shoes. One advantage of this method of construction, compared with moulding a rubber sole, is that high temperatures are not required. The number of operations involved for the newer methods of construction is very much smaller than for the traditional methods. For example, one operation for the injection moulded construction takes the place of about 30 separate operations required for the goodyear welted method, although the product is not, of course, identical.

Table 3.3. Method of construction of shoes made in the British Isles

	Percentage of total	
	1957	1962
Cemented	40	51
Goodyear welted	15	9
Machine sewn	13	4
Veldschoen	13	7
Low-pressure vulcanised	10	12
High-pressure vulcanised	4	11
Injection moulded	—	1
Other	5	5
	100	100

Source: British United Shoe Machinery Company.

The costs of the machinery used in the making department may account for as much as sixty per cent of the total machine costs of a shoe factory, and the utilisation of the capacity of these machines is therefore important. The output capacity of the machines used varies, and this involves a problem of balancing the output of the set of machines. An example of the problems involved in achieving a balanced set of machines is provided by some calculations made of labour utilisation in a making department for manufacturing women's cemented shoes. These calculations are shown in table 3.4 below.

The second column of the table shows the daily output of an operative working on each type of operation. Output per day varies from 480 to 2,400 pairs according to the operation. The third column shows the number of operatives performing each operation who would be required to make 1,200 pairs per day. This is given in terms of fractions of operatives, and provides an estimate of the output per man of a perfectly balanced set of machines and operatives. The remaining columns provide estimates of the number of operatives required at varying levels of output when fractions of operatives are excluded.

The highest possible level of productivity, given the capacity output for each operation, would be 60 pairs per day per operative. With an output of 600 pairs a day production would be 29 pairs a day per operative, and with an output of 1,200 pairs a day production would be 46 pairs per operative. At 1,500 pairs productivity would be lower than at 1,200, because the capacity of nearly half the machines is grouped in this range. At 2,400 pairs productivity would be up to 50 pairs per operative, and at 9,600 pairs (not shown in the table) it would be 55 pairs.

Such calculations as these exaggerate the effects of achieving a balance of operations, however. In practice the skill of operatives varies, and it may be possible to position the most skilful operatives on machines which are tending to cause bottlenecks. It was found by comparing productivity on various operations at a number of factories that the faster operatives were up to three times as fast as the slowest.[1] The foreman of a large lasting room has estimated that the variation about the average output on a machine in his lasting room was 20 per cent either way. Other ways of achieving balance are provided by the possibility of adjusting the operations or the method of making the shoe, or by having one operative performing two operations, or by some operatives working overtime. In small factories it may be economic to substitute hand operations for some machine operations.

Table 3.5 gives another example of the problem of balancing the output of machines. It shows the number of machines required in the making, finishing, and shoe rooms of factories where leather-soled goodyear welted shoes are made.

In general, the machines used in the making room can be rapidly adjusted to make different styles and sizes. One exception to this general rule is vulcanising plant. The output of the individual vulcanising units is not very great, as the rubber for the sole has to be set in a mould and this takes from five to ten minutes. Thus each unit, which usually has two moulds for a pair of shoes, produces between 50 and 100 pairs during an eight-hour day. It takes a matter of hours to adjust the size of shoe which the moulds are set to make, and this means that, to avoid adjusting the machines at all, a whole battery of units is required. But provided long runs of each size of shoe can be made, the use of a limited number of these machines would not result in any serious financial handicap.

The machines used in the making room are arranged in the order in which operations have to be performed, and groups of the relatively low-capacity machines are placed together to balance productive capacity. The parts, and eventually the complete shoes, are transported either on trolleys which can be passed on as each operation is performed, or on

---

(1) J. R. Manning and L. Sychrava, A Comparison of the Direct Costs of Moulded on and Welted Shoes (p. 8). An unpublished research report.

Table 3.4. Labour utilisation in a making room

Operation	Output per day per operative in pairs	Theoretical no. of operatives per 1,200 pairs per day	Possible number of operatives for a daily output of pairs					
			600	800	1000	1200	1500	2400
1	1800	0.7	1	1	1	1	1	2
2	1440	0.8	1	1	1	1	2	2
3	1260	1.0	1	1	1	1	2	2
4 (1)	1800	0.7	1	1	1	1	1	2
5	1260	1.0	1	1	1	1	2	2
6 (1)	480	2.5	2	2	3	3	4	5
7	600	2.0	1	2	2	2	3	4
8 (1)	1440	0.8	1	1	1	1	2	2
9	1860	0.6	1	1	1	1	1	2
10	1980	0.6	1	1	1	1	1	2
11	840	1.4	1	1	1	2	2	3
12	1860	0.6	1	1	1	1	1	2
13	1320	0.9	1	1	1	1	2	2
14	1860	0.6	1	1	1	1	1	2
15	1200	1.0	1	1	1	1	2	2
16	1200	1.0	1	1	1	1	2	2
17 (1)	720	1.7	1	2	2	2	3	4
18	1200	1.0	1	1	1	1	2	2
19	960	0.7	1	1	2	2	2	3
20	2400	0.5	1	1	1	1	1	1
Total number of operatives		20.1	21	23	25	26	37	48
Output (pairs) per operative day		60	29	35	40	46	41	50

(1) Expensive machines which should be fully loaded

Source: Adapted from table given in 'The Streamlining of Shoe Production', a paper given at the 1962 Annual Conference of the British Boot and Shoe Institution, by D. Grimwade and J. Bunten.

Table 3.5. The number of machines required and scale

Daily output (in pairs)	Number of machines	Machines per pair per day
200	41	.205
400	43	.108
600	50	.083
800	55	.071
1000	61	.061
1500	83	.055
2000	106	.053

Source: J. R. Manning and L. Sychrava,
A Comparison of Direct Costs
of Moulded-on and Welted Shoes, (p. 33)

a conveyor belt from which each shoe is lifted off individually for each operation and then replaced. Alternatively, trolleys with batches of shoes may be attached to a conveyor track to be moved between operatives.

There is no need for a finishing room for the new methods of shoe construction, but the goodyear welted construction requires a large finishing room, where shoe bottoms are trimmed, coloured and waxed. The shoe room is a relatively small department in which shoes are inspected and prepared for despatch. In addition to the departments described above, there are service departments for storing materials, costing, personnel, buying and selling, but only in large factories are they distinguished, and some of them are organised on a firm rather than a factory basis.

Cost analysis

Table 3.6. gives an approximate breakdown of costs for the manufacture of cheap men's shoes. Information obtained from firms manufacturing women's shoes shows that the percentage breakdown of the costs of production for medium-price women's shoes is approximately the same. The table illustrates the importance of the cost of materials, which amount to 60 per cent of the manufacturer's costs of production and, compared with many industries, the unimportance of the costs of machinery. Most manufacturers insist that profits as a percentage of turnover are small and that profits in the shoe industry are concentrated at the retailing end. If shoes are sold through a wholesaler he receives a discount of about 6 per cent on the manufacturer's price.

Table 3.6. Cost breakdown for men's cheap shoes (1962)

	Shillings	Percentage of manufacturer's price	Percentage of price to the customer
Materials	16	60	40
Direct labour	5	18	12
Depreciation and rentals of machinery	1	4	$2\frac{1}{2}$
Manufacturer's overheads and profits	5	18	$12\frac{1}{2}$
	27	100	$67\frac{1}{2}$
Purchase tax	1		$2\frac{1}{2}$
Distribution costs and retailer's profit	12		30
Retail price	40		100

Table 3.7 gives a breakdown of labour and machine costs by departments for two factories. The estimates shown in the columns marked (a) are based on information received from several factories making women's shoes. The data in column (b) refer to the manufacture of men's goodyear welted shoes, and indicates the greater relative importance of labour costs in the making and finishing departments for this type of production.

Table 3.7. Labour and machine costs by department

Department	Direct labour costs as percentage of total direct labour costs		Machine costs as a percentage of total machine costs	Machine costs as a percentage of direct labour costs
	(a)	(b)	(a)	(a)
Clicking	14	13	15	24
Closing	45	23	10	5
Preparation	10	7	6	13
Making	23	44 (1)	64	61
Shoe	8	13	5	9
	100	100	100	22

(1) Including the finishing room.

Many factories frequently operate well below full capacity because of seasonal and cyclical fluctuations in trade. As demand declines both labour and machine capacity are underutilised. The labour force can be adjusted, but it is the general experience that operatives spread out the work available when output declines and, in any case, a fall in output presents a problem of balancing operations which makes it impossible to reduce the labour force in proportion to the fall in output. The extent of the rise in unit direct labour costs which results from a decline in demand will also be partly determined by the willingness of management to lay off employees, and the proportion of employees paid on a piece-rate basis. But the significance of the difference between time- and piece-rate payment is limited, at a time of low output, because the wages of operatives paid on a piece-rate basis have to be made up to a guaranteed minimum.

One cause of rising short-term unit production costs when output falls is the stability of overheads. Estimates of the division of 'overheads' between fixed and variable differ. In practice at least 50 per cent of the overheads are fixed in the short run, and the percentage may be as high as 70 per cent. Assuming that both direct labour costs and overheads are 50 per cent fixed and 50 per cent variable in the short run, then costs of production for varying levels of output for a factory with a capacity of 1,200 pairs a day would be as shown in table 3.8. With an output of 600 pairs a day or half capacity, unit labour and overheads would be 50 per cent higher, and total unit costs of production would be 20 per cent higher than with an output equal to 'normal' capacity. In the short run capacity is usually determined by the capacity of the closing room, although a critical bottleneck could occur elsewhere.

Table 3.8. Unit short run costs and the level of capacity working

Output—pairs per day	Cost of materials	Direct labour and overheads	Total production costs
(Total Unit Production Costs for Output of 1,200 pairs a day = 100)			
1,200	60	40	100
1,000	60	44	104
800	60	50	110
600	60	60	120

The relationship between factory size and unit costs: I

To simplify the consideration of the long run relationship between unit costs and output our first estimates refer to a hypothetical factory making one style of shoe. We have assumed that the factory makes a range of fittings and sizes of one style of medium-price women's cemented court shoes, and that production is organised in long runs

of each fitting and size. It is also assumed that the factory works to
capacity as nearly as possible, that the price of materials used is not
affected by the level of output, and that the most efficient methods of
production are used at each scale of output.

Table 3.9 gives an estimate of relative unit production costs at various
levels of capacity output. These estimates, which are intended as an
approximate indication of the magnitude of economies, are based on the
costs and methods of production used in a number of factories which
produce a diversity of styles. First copy costs are ignored, since if
one style of shoe were made indefinitely these would be insignificant.
Column 2 shows the economies in labour and overhead costs and column 3 shows the effect of these economies when the cost of materials,
which is assumed not to be affected by the scale of output, is included.
The cost of materials is assumed to be 55 per cent of total production
costs for a factory with a capacity of 300 pairs a day.

Table 3.9. Output capacity and unit production costs

(1)	(2)	(3)
Output capacity pairs per day	Labour and overheads	Total production costs, including materials
300	100	100
600	94	97
1,200	90	95.5
2,400	87	94
4,800	85	93

The estimates show economies, at a diminishing rate, up to a level of
production of 4,800 pairs a day. There are no clear reasons for supposing that economies of scale would stop or be reversed at this level,
but above it economies would be small. These calculations are based
on the assumption that the machinery used in factories making a diversity of styles would also be used in a factory making one style. If in
fact, however, a number of factories were each to be devoted to making
one style of shoe, it is possible that new high-capacity machinery would
be developed which would increase the economies of large-scale production.

Considering the departments of a shoe factory in turn, the economies
of scale for a clicking room would be negligible. The output of a press
clicker is about 125 pairs a day depending on his skill and the overtime
he works, and there are few advantages to be achieved by dividing the
clicking operations. In the closing department, in which heavy direct
labour costs are incurred, economies of scale would also be small. It
would be necessary for some operatives to perform more than one
operation if output were less than 1,200 pairs a day, and even above

this level of output there would be scope for dividing operations. But if we assume that one style is made, and that there are long runs of each fitting and size, this would not materially increase costs.

For the purpose of making these estimates it is assumed that factories with a low level of capacity would buy-out soles and heels ready made. If soles had to be cut, and heels covered or sprayed etc., there would be clear economies of scale in the preparation room for factories up to an output of at least 3,000 pairs per day. However, the possibility of buying-out limits the disadvantages that a small factory would suffer in the preparation department.

The main economies of scale occur in the making room. The problem of balancing machinery and the methods of partially offsetting this have been described above. As we have seen, progressively smaller economies above an output of about 1,200 pairs a day would occur as a result of balancing operations.

In this industry the type of machinery used for most operations is not affected by the size of output, and higher levels of output are achieved by duplicating machines where necessary. The development of machines with higher capacity has been limited by the variable quality of leather and the need in practice to make a variety of styles and sizes. However, apart from the problem of balancing machines and operations, larger factories have an advantage because of their greater flexibility. If there are machine breakdowns, or employees are absent, there is more scope for adjustment by overtime working and by demanding a special effort from the remainder of the operatives.

We have assumed in this example that output is all of one style. In these unrealistic circumstances control and có-ordination of production would be straightforward. In factories with an output of less than about 1,200 pairs a day the foremen of departments would probably have time to spare from supervision, but any diseconomies caused by this can be partially offset by the foremen acting, at least part-time, as operatives. This was in fact the practice in some of the departments of the factories visited.

We also assumed that the prices paid for materials would not be affected by scale. In practice, scale would determine the bargaining strength of the manufacturer against the tanners. This, together with the fact that the delivery and sales costs of tanners and other suppliers would be lower for large orders, would give an advantage to the large manufacturer. In comparing a manufacturer with an output of 300 pairs a day and one with 4,800, this difference might amount in practice to 6 per cent of material costs, or $3\frac{1}{2}$ per cent of total production costs. Even above an output of 4,800 shoes a day there is probably some scope for economies of scale in buying, but these will be limited. The larger-scale manufacturers buy their leather from several tanners, and the scope for economies will depend on the negotiating strength of the manufacturer rather than real economies to the suppliers. Large-scale manufacturers may also achieve an advantage by being able to enter into direct negotiations with foreign tanners.

The estimates refer to factories making women's medium price, cemented court shoes, but it is thought that the estimates are also broadly correct for other types of manufacture. The breakdown of costs shown in table 3.7 indicates that making-room costs represent a higher proportion of total production costs in the manufacture of men's shoes by the goodyear welted method. It is in the making department that the scope for economies of scale is most marked, and we should therefore expect that economies of scale would be slightly greater for the manufacture of men's shoes by this method. Also there are grounds for supposing that the economies associated with a high level of output, as measured by pairs produced, are more marked for the production of children's shoes than for women's.

On the basis of the artificial assumption than one style is made, economies of scale for high-pressure vulcanising would tend to be slightly smaller than for cemented construction, because the individual vulcanising units have a relatively small output—about 150 pairs during three eight-hour shifts. The adjustment of vulcanising units by replacing the moulds would not significantly affect costs because it can be assumed that long runs of each size and fitting would be made. New machines for injection moulding of plastic soles are being introduced into the industry. These machines have an output capacity of about 1,500 pairs a day and, compared with vulcanising units, confer a distinct advantage for large-scale units. Also machines for moulding complete plastic shoes are being used with an output of 2,000 pairs a day. Economies of large-scale production for this type of construction are clearly greater than for other types of construction.

The quality of shoe made also affects the economies of scale. It is generally agreed in the industry that quality is partly dependent on the time taken to perform operations. A high-quality shoe takes longer to make, and therefore entails lower productivity per man and per machine in terms of pairs of shoes produced. This means that economies operate over a lower range of output.

The relationship between factory size and unit costs: II

So far we have assumed that one style of shoe is produced. What is the effect of dropping this assumption? Clearly costs of production per pair are increased by manufacturing a range of styles, but it is particularly difficult to quantify these additional costs because of the varying degree of difference between styles. A change of style may involve only a minor alteration in the closing department or in the clicking and closing departments. Alternatively different styles may entail different lasts. For example, shoes with pointed toes are made on a last of different shape from those with square toes. If different methods of construction are required, some additional machines are needed in the making room, but in practice many factories, especially small factories, concentrate on one type of construction.

In the book-printing industry we found that the first copy costs were of considerable importance in the overall costs of printing. In the footwear industry they are of much less significance. The main 'first copy' costs for a new style of shoe are the cost of the design, of making sample shoes and clicking patterns, and of a set of lasts if these are required. If the design, samples, and patterns for hand clicking are bought out the cost may be of the order of £70 for a new style. Some of the firms visited employed their own designers and cut their own patterns, but for none of the firms visited did the costs of designing and preparing samples and patterns amount to more than 10 per cent of labour and overhead costs, and for some it was less than 5 per cent. If new lasts are required for a new style this is usually the most important first copy cost. Lasts may cost as much as £2 per pair, and if the shoes are of welted construction they may have to remain on the last for up to four days, depending on their quality. For some types of construction the time on the last is much shorter: at one factory making cemented shoes the shoes were on the last for less than an hour. In this case, of course, the number of lasts required for a given level of production per day is much smaller. Most of the machines used in shoemaking do not require adjustment for a change of styles and so there are in general no 'make-ready' costs, but an exception to this rule is vulcanising equipment. If a change of style involves a change in the shape of the sole of the shoe different moulds are required.

The method of construction affects the first copy costs, but the frequency with which the range of styles is changed also affects the method of construction. For example, where frequent changes of style are made the cemented construction is more appropriate than the vulcanised construction. Also, one firm may make use of one last shape, to make a series of styles, for which another firm would use more than one last in order to achieve higher quality. In addition, firms limit their range of styles to fit in with their method of construction and stock of lasts.

It is not possible to separate the diseconomies of making a range of styles from the length of production runs. If we define a production run as the number of pairs of a style made before switching to another style, then, for a given output, the length of production run will tend to vary inversely with the number of styles made. There are other factors determining the length of runs, such as the scope for forecasting sales of each style, the ability to finance stocks, and the size of the stock of lasts. In practice, many manufacturers normally make for orders, and manufacture for stock only when insufficient orders are available. In boom phases of the cycle they can group orders together to lengthen production runs, but at other times there is less incentive to do this as a grouping of orders to obtain longer production runs would increase the problem of surplus stocks.

The most important effect of short production runs is the reduction in labour productivity. It is found that the longer the run the higher the output and quality achieved by the operatives, and this improved quality of work enables the costs of supervision and inspection to be reduced. Difficulty in balancing operations as styles change also causes a loss of potential output. Another important diseconomy of short production runs is the cost of planning to ensure that the right parts for shoes are assembled at the right time and place, and that the sequence of production runs and operations on each style minimise any loss of productivity caused by lack of balance.

The length of production runs also affects the organisation of production. If production runs are short, it is sometimes desirable to divide the production lines in some departments, such as the closing and the making room, particularly in cases where different methods of construction and last shapes are used. Departments are sub-divided in this way in many large factories. The advantages of this procedure are that it extends the length of production runs for individual operatives for operations which are duplicated if a single production line is used, that it facilitates the balancing of operations and that it reduces the losses caused by hold-ups etc.

From our discussions with the managers of shoe factories it is clear that economies of long production runs are of more practical importance in this industry than the relationship between the total output of a factory and unit costs. These economies are particularly difficult to quantify because differences of style cover anything from the addition of a strap to a different method of construction. An accountant with experience of a medium- and a large-scale firm of footwear manufacturers, estimated that if the average length of production run were increased from 200 to 6,000 pairs—all of one construction—with an equivalent reduction in the variety of styles, the saving in unit labour and overhead costs would be of the order of 10 to 15 per cent. These reductions in cost represent 4 to 6 per cent of the total cost of production per pair if material costs are assumed not to be affected. In practice the cost of leather would be affected, and this would add another 1 to 2 per cent to the saving. A manufacturer with average runs of about 1,000 pairs doubted whether there were in practice significant economies to be achieved by doubling the length of production run from 1,000 to 2,000 pairs, but agreed that significant economies could be achieved by increasing the length of production run up to a level of about 1,000 pairs.

What effect does the manufacture of a range of styles have on our estimates of the economies associated with varying levels of output for factories making one style of shoe? If we assume that factories make a small range of styles, for example of men's shoes of traditional styles, all of one construction, the estimates would not be greatly affected. If we assume that a wide range of styles is made, and that for market reasons this increases in proportion to the output of the factory—for example the production of quality fashion shoes—the possible economies of scale would be much reduced. This would apply especially for factories with a total output of more than 1,200 pairs a day, since the potential economies of dividing and balancing operations, which are considerable at this scale if the range of styles made is small, would be reduced, and there would be none of the other advantages accruing from longer production runs.

If a large number of styles is made, and the number of styles is not affected by the total output of the factory (this could apply to firms making medium-price men's and women's shoes), larger factories would then have the advantage of longer production runs and higher outputs of each style and would enable economies of scale to be reconciled with variety.

One possible diseconomy for large factories making a wide range of styles is the cost of management, but we have been unable to test this. The scale at which it is no longer possible for a manager to supervise all departments depends on the type of production, the range of styles made, and the abilities of the manager. If a wide range of styles is made, an output of about 1,200 pairs a day is regarded by some managers as about the right level. Above it, the difficulties of control may affect any economies to be achieved by a better balance of operations. However, diseconomies can be circumvented by dividing departments and, if necessary, a whole factory. If this happens there should still be scope for some economies by grouping similar styles together and so reducing the variation of styles on individual production lines.

Many small factories in the industry are run efficiently by a manager with a minimum of secretarial assistance. In this industry, as in others, as firms expand the number of specialist staff grows more than proportionately. A large firm employs personnel managers, planners, advertising managers, education officers and designers etc. whereas in a small business the sole manager often combines all these roles with his management responsibilities. One of the reasons why the managers, often the owners, of small firms can do this successfully, is that they are willing to devote a great deal of time and effort to the job and have the enthusiasm and the incentive that salaried managers often lack. In practice, the character of many shoe-manufacturing units is inextricably bound up with that of the manager/owner. It is worth noting that though the quality of management is important in this industry it is not the size of factories per se which creates difficulties of management but the variation in styles. For large factories which produce a small range of styles the task of management is relatively straightforward, and the costs of management do not act as a diseconomy of scale.

A further advantage of a large firm is that it may be able to achieve economies in selling costs, and only a large firm can finance a national advertising campaign to establish a public demand for its shoes. One company has recently been successful in selling a standard range of men's shoes in large quantities partly because of an advertising campaign.(1) Another field in which a large firm can achieve an advantage is in research on new methods of production. The cost of research can be spread over a greater output and experiments in introducing new methods are relatively less risky. For example, a new conveyor can be tried out in one factory, and, if successful, can then be adopted in other factories.

---

(1) The company referred to introduced a new method of vulcanising rubber soles at about the same time as an advertising campaign to sell a standardised range of shoes was started. It is thus difficult to distinguish in this case between success caused by standardisation, by technical development, and by advertising.

In the footwear industry, all these advantages of large firms are to some extent offset. A small firm can concentrate on a limited section of the market, and sell its products through a wholesaler or direct to a multiple chain of shops or a mail-order firm. In this way it can avoid the selling costs of presenting a limited range of products to independent retailers. To some extent retailers, and particularly multiple chains, advertise for the small manufacturers who make their products, thus offsetting the fact that they cannot afford to advertise themselves. S. A. T. R. A. (1) provides research facilities for all its members, and the shoe machinery manufacturers provide some research facilities and technical assistance which the small manufacturer can use. Management consultants can also provide specialist advice on organisation and work study. Large firms can employ separate design staff, but it is doubtful whether this confers an important advantage. The smaller firms can buy-out designs, and managers aided by discussions on design in trade papers can produce their own designs.

Some firms in the industry operate more than one factory. One firm operates more than ten—indeed the fact that firms operate more than one factory tends to indicate that the economies of scale for individual factories are limited. The recent practice of large shoe manufacturers in the U.S. of building new small factories indicates that the division of output between factories is not determined by the historical development of firms alone. The main economy of production costs for a multi-factory firm, compared with small firms operating single factories, is that each factory can concentrate on a limited number of styles.

There are two factors which tend to reduce the economies of scale for the manufacturer in this country. One is the fact that many of the machines used in the industry are rented. The British United Shoe Machinery Co. supplies a high proportion of the machines used by firms in the industry, and, although it is no longer the policy of the company to insist on hiring out as opposed to selling its machinery, many manufacturers still rent the bulk of their machinery. There are two bases for fixing rents: a fixed rent and/or a rent varying with the level of output. Some machines carry no variable rent, whereas others carry a variable rent which works out at four to five times the fixed rent. Because of the variable rent a factory using its plant to the optimum loses part of the potential advantage of lower machine costs. The other factor limiting economies of scale is the payment of operatives by piece rates. This system of payment is widely but not universally used in the industry, and to some extent results in the more efficient firms paying higher wages per man, although not of course per pair of shoes made. These factors reducing the economies of scale and specialisation do not however have a significant effect on the conclusions reached above.

---

(1) The Shoe and Allied Trades Research Association.

Other evidence relating to the economies of scale, and conclusions

The structure of the industry was outlined at the beginning of this chapter. The large number of small establishments which operate in the industry are compatible with our estimates of small economies of scale in the industry, in the sense that economies tail off at relatively small scales of output. Data obtained from the British Footwear Manufacturers Association indicate, however, that over the past ten years the concentration of the industry has increased. Small firms have left the industry, particularly in some sections of the industry such as heavy boot manufacture, other small firms have amalgamated or been taken over by larger firms, and there has been a reduction in both the number of small firms and small factories operating in the industry.

We have obtained data to compare the structure of the industry in this country with that in the U.S.A. and in some other European countries. These data indicate that the size of manufacturing units is not very different in these other countries. Relatively small-scale manufacturing units are clearly able to survive in the industry, in spite of the growth in concentration that has been noted.

In 1944, H. A. Silverman (1) reached the qualified conclusion that a complete team of modern and well-balanced machines, together with the necessary complement of operatives, works to normal capacity if it produces 1,000 to 1,200 pairs a day, and that the number of operatives employed in such a unit would vary from approximately 250 to 350, according to different conditions. The main change since the time when Silverman made his study has been an increase in labour productivity in the industry. Though the normal capacity of a balanced set of machines, if a wide range of styles is made, has only risen from 1,000-1,200 to 1,200-1,400 pairs a day, productivity per man has increased substantially, and a full complement of operatives for many types of production would not now be more than 100. Part of this increase in productivity has been caused because many more components are now bought out. Other factors are improvements in the scope of operations performed by machines, better planning of production, and improvements in the quality of materials e.g. the introduction of quick setting cement.

J. S. Bain, (2) writing about conditions in the United States at the beginning of the 1950's, and basing his estimates on a questionnaire sent to manufacturers, found that the minimum optimum factory scale ran from 2,500 to 10,000 pairs per day. At smaller scales of output, estimates of the potential economies of scale ranged from quite small to moderate. Bain reported a study by Mr. Bruce Cheek who placed the minimum optimum plant scale for men's shoes at 2,400 pairs per day, with the qualification that for low-priced men's shoes the minimum optimum might go as high as 6,000 pair per day. Bain also referred to industry

---

(1) H. A. Silverman, Studies in Industrial Organisation, p. 215

(2) J. S. Bain, Barriers to New Competition, Cambridge. Mass. 1956, p. 230.

sources which place the minimum optimum as low as 2,400 pairs per day only for high priced men's shoes or for women's shoes, and estimate the minimum optimum to be typically in the neighbourhood of 4,000 to 5,000 pairs per day otherwise. These estimates are not incompatible with our estimates.

The Committee on Industrial Organisation in Ireland, in its report on the leather footwear industry, published in 1962, emphasised the probable effects of the introduction of new machinery and new materials, such as plastics for uppers and conveyor belt assembly lines, for increasing the advantages of large-scale plants in the industry. It also expressed doubts about the future viability of small manufacturing plants with less than 100 employees. The effect of these developments applies as much to British as to Irish manufacturers.

The use of plastic as a material for uppers in place of leather may have more impact on the economies of scale than the other developments mentioned. The uniform quality of plastic material may make the automation of clicking departments feasible if long runs of shoes can be made. Clearly the introduction of plastics will reduce the cost of materials in relation to labour and other costs, and this alone will increase the relative importance of the economies of scale in manufacturing.

The main developments in machinery have been to increase the scope of the operations performed by each machine. This trend does not significantly affect the economies of scale, if scale is measured in terms of output, nor does the speeding up of the manufacturing cycle which has been achieved. The further development of new methods of constructing shoes may, however, increase economies of scale for certain types of production, especially if long runs for styles can be arranged.

The dimensions of scale for the footwear industry which we have discussed are the length of production runs, the range of styles, the number of production lines and the output of factories and firms. All these dimensions of scale are interrelated. For a hypothetical factory making a single style of shoe, economies of scale would continue up to an output of about 4,800 pairs a day. Above this level they would be low. A daily output of this size is small in relation to the output of the industry: it represents about 1 per cent of the total U.K. output of shoes with leather uppers. Where it is necessary for market reasons to manufacture a wide range of styles, but total factory output is limited, the economies of scale would be smaller because of the problems of balancing operations and controlling production. However, where large factories make a range of styles, they often have the advantage of long production runs and can hence reap appreciable economies of scale.

In practice the main advantage of large firms in this industry is their ability to produce fewer styles in relation to their output. In so far as a firm can expand its output without increasing the range of styles it makes, and without reducing its prices, it can achieve substantial advantages from the economies of scale. However, small manufacturers can limit the range of styles they make by marketing arrangements, and this can considerably reduce their disadvantage. Where the total market for certain types of footwear is limited,the small-scale manufacturer can compete. In any case,economies of scale are only one of the forces determining the profitability of a footwear manufacturing business: the control of retail outlets and the ability to forecast changes in taste for different styles of shoe can be of decisive importance for a manufacturer.

During recent years the concentration of the industry has increased both in terms of factories and firms. Our estimates indicate that such a concentration of manufacturing capacity should provide economies, especially where there is scope for rationalising the number of styles made, and our impression is that there is room for further concentration in the industry as a means of reducing costs.

A factor which should operate to increase production runs, and hence the economies of scale, is the continuing concentration of retail outlets. This concentration is probably as important for achieving a limitation of the number of styles made by each manufacturer as further amalgamations of manufacturing units would be.

4   Steel Production

Introduction

There are three main groups of operations involved in the production of steel. The conversion of iron ore to pig iron in a blast furnace, the conversion of pig iron to steel in a steel furnace, and the 'finishing' of steel by rolling, forging, or casting.(1) In an integrated works, where iron ore is converted to finished steel products, there are also subsidiary process units such as coke ovens and plant for preparing and sintering iron ore and for producing oxygen.

Whether measured by sales, value added, employment or investment, the steel industry is one of the largest U.K. manufacturing industries. In all there are 262 companies(2) engaged in making steel, in 310 plants, employing about 300, 000 people, but only 23 of the 310 plants are integrated works. Of the remainder, 37 cover both steelmaking and finishing, and 250 works specialise on one group of operations, mainly finishing operations. Although there are 262 companies operating in the industry, it is nevertheless dominated by a small number of large companies and nine companies produce about 80 per cent of the total U.K. output of crude steel. In addition to this concentration, the large companies tend, with a few exceptions, of which the United Steel Companies is the best known, to specialise in making a general category of finished steel products such as sheet and strip, or pipes and tubes, or heavy plates and sections or wire rods and bars.

During recent years great technological changes have occurred in the industry, especially in the field of steelmaking using the oxygen processes, and the effect of these developments on the structure of the industry and on its costs have only just begun to show. In the earlier post-war period other changes in methods and techniques employed were taking place, such as the preparation of the iron ore before charging it

------

(1) For readers without a knowledge of the processes used in the industry Appendix 7 of the Iron and Steel Board's Special Report, 1964, on Development in the Iron and Steel Industry, gives a thumb-nail description of the main processes used in the industry. The Iron and Steel Federation have published 'A simple guide to basic processes in the Iron and Steel Industry' and more comprehensive descriptions can be obtained from textbooks on steel technology.

(2) The British Iron and Steel Federation 1964—Steel—Leave Well Alone, p. 7.

into the blast furnace, the sintering of the blast-furnace burden, the use of 'self-fluxing' materials for blast furnaces, and the semi-automatic control of rolling operations. A consequence of all these technical changes is that attempts to estimate the effect of the scale of output on production costs, by collecting data over a period during which the scale of output of a plant has increased, are vitiated by the lack of comparability of production techniques. Similarly, comparisons between different plants, at any one moment of time, are made very difficult. Since both the time series and the cross-sectional methods of estimating economies of scale are unsatisfactory, we have looked to engineering estimates for evidence of economies of scale in the steel industry. This method has involved us in a search for cost analyses of the type which are sometimes made by a company when it is considering a scheme of expansion. Normally there is some output figure taken as a datum for expansion schemes, but such figures are often estimates with a margin of flexibility, so that it is sensible for companies to investigate what operating and capital costs would be at levels of output both below and in excess of the projected level. We have also made use of similar estimates made by the staff of the Iron and Steel Board, and also by engineering consultants, who are sometimes asked to advise on the most suitable plant and equipment when firms are planning to expand their capacity. In addition, we have referred to engineering-type studies which have already been published.

Our interest in economies of scale has been in respect of particular items of plant and of complete works. The inter-relationship of the items of plant in iron- and steel-making has the economic corollary that economies of scale in respect of, say, blast furnaces or a particular type of rolling mill, cannot be considered in isolation but must be looked at in the light of the cost structure of the total complex of plant. For example, the fact that rolling is a continuous process, and that it follows the batch process of steelmaking, is one of the constraints on the unlimited growth in the size of steelmaking furnaces. The cycle time of the steelmaking process is virtually constant, irrespective of the size of the vessel used, and the steel has to be maintained at a high temperature between the completion of each batch or 'heat'. Thus a diseconomy of large steel furnaces is the cost of heating the steel waiting to be rolled. Although we have looked first at items of plant in isolation, since it is obviously of interest to know the relationship between scale and cost for individual processes, we have gone on to build up a complete picture of the economies of scale for an integrated plant.

The economies of scale in making pig iron, steelmaking and finishing are examined separately in the following three sections of the chapter. The costs of handling materials are considered in a separate section, and the economies of scale for integrated plants are described in the penultimate section, which also includes a breakdown of costs of steelmaking. The structure of the industry is outlined in the final section and related to our estimates of the economies of scale. In all sections of this chapter there are unavoidable gaps in our figures, but we have done our best not to leave serious ones.

It may help to put our estimates into perspective if we give here a rough measure of the proportion of the costs of steel manufacture accounted for by different processes. Excluding the costs of materials, ironmaking accounts for some 29 per cent of the operating and capital costs for an integrated works, steelmaking for 25 per cent and rolling for 46 per cent. These estimates relate to an integrated works with a capacity of one million tons per annum. Such a breakdown of costs depends upon the type of steel products made.

Ironmaking

There are several ways of producing iron from iron ore, but an overwhelmingly high proportion of iron is made in blast furnaces. For markets as large as that provided by the U.K. and for the relative fuel costs ruling in the U.K. the other methods are not at present economic. The average size of blast furnace has risen continuously during the past 50 years, and the use of new techniques such as ore preparation and oxygen enrichment have further increased the productive capacity of blast furnaces.

The capital cost of blast furnaces,(1) quoted by one manufacturer, per ton of annual output in 1952, fell from £8 5s. in the case of 18' 0" hearth diameter furnaces to £7 8s. for 21'6" hearth diameter furnaces and £7 3s. for 29' 0" diameter furnaces. In each case, the costs are based on a plant to produce 900, 000 tons of iron p.a. which would require four 18' furnaces, three 21' 6" or two 29' furnaces.

An engineering estimate made in 1962 of the comparative capital costs of a plant to produce 100, 000 and 1, 000, 000 tons per year (excluding civil engineering, transport and spares costs) gave the cost per annual ton as £12.1 for the 100, 000 ton p.a. plant and £5.6 for the 1, 000, 000 tons p.a. plant. This reduction results from a combination of the advantages of furnaces with larger dimensions and the savings in cost per ton of associated equipment. For this estimate it was assumed that the 100, 000 ton plant would consist of one blast furnace and that the million ton plant would consist of two larger furnaces. Blast furnaces are being constructed with a capacity of more than a million tons a year, but the flexibility achieved by having two furnaces was considered more important than the economies to be achieved by installing only one. It takes about three months to reline a furnace, and this has to be done approximately every three years. It is for such periods that the installation of more than one furnace is required to provide some flexibility.

Coke consumption, labour and maintenance costs, per ton of pig iron produced, also fall as the size of furnace increases. Two of the main factors affecting the costs of production of a blast furnace are the driving rate and the coke rate. The driving rate is the amount of coke that can be burned per unit of time, and the coke rate is the amount of coke needed to produce a ton of iron. The driving rate increases and the coke rate falls as the size of furnace rises. However, one offsetting cost for larger furnaces is the cost of preparing raw materials, agglomerating fine par-

---

(1) Excluding the cost of ore preparation plant and power station equipment.

ticles of ore (sintering), or forming the ore into pellets. These processes are essential for the efficient operation of large furnaces and would also improve the coke rate for small furnaces, but are not usually considered economic in their case.

The sizes of plant assumed in the comparison of capital costs mentioned above, i.e. plants producing 100,000 tons p.a. and one million tons per annum, were also used in a comparison of operating costs. The same usage of iron ore and fluxes per ton of iron was taken in both cases, but it was calculated that the coke rate would be much lower in the larger plant, due to pretreatment of the ore (mainly by sintering), high top pressure, fuel injection, oxygen enrichment and humidification of the blast. These aids are technically feasible in the case of the smaller furnace also, but it is very doubtful whether they would be economic for a plant to produce 100,000 tons a year, and the comparison below assumes that they would not be used in this case. Thus for the 100,000 tons p.a. plant the coke rate is taken as 1.125 tons, and in the case of the 1,000,000 tons p.a. plant as 0.8 tons per ton of iron.(1)

Two furnaces to produce a million tons a year require more men to operate and maintain them than the single small furnace required for a 100,000 tons p.a. plant, but it was estimated that labour costs per ton would be about 40 per cent lower for the million ton p.a. plant than for the smaller plant. For similar reasons maintenance costs per ton fall. The comparative operating costs per ton for ironmaking, including materials and excluding administration, amortisation, gas and slag credits come to £10.7 (100,000 tons p.a. size) and £8.8 (1,000,000 tons p.a. size). If we add to operating costs 20 per cent of the estimated capital costs, as an annual charge for both depreciation and return on capital, the estimate for the 100,000 tons p.a. plant is £13.2 per ton and for the 1,000,000 tons p.a. plant £10.0 per ton, giving a saving of 25 per cent for the smaller plant.

The figures have been taken from estimates made with the express purpose of establishing an integrated steelworks, technically suitable for operation in an emergent country with a shortage of capital, skilled labour and management. As a corollary of that, the plant has been specified with the deliberate intention of cutting out, at the smaller scale, all those items of equipment which have over the years been uncritically assumed to be necessary, but which on certain assumptions, such as an unlimited supply of (admittedly unskilled) labour, can be dispensed with. This was done in order to minimise the effect of economies of scale on the estimated relative price of steel from small steelworks. A similar comparison, which assumed the conditions of a developed country for both the small- and large-scale plant, would undoubtedly show greater economies of scale.

---

(1) These coke rates are high by U.K. standards for new plants.

A recent comparison of costs excluding materials for hypothetical blast-furnace plants of different sizes has been made by the Economic Commission for Latin America. (1) It shows the following trend of costs per ton:

100,000 tons p.a.	200,000 tons p.a.	500,000 tons p.a.	1,000,000 tons p.a.	1,500,000 tons p.a.
131	100	71	58	52

The saving in costs per ton for a million-ton plant compared with a plant to produce 100,000 tons is 56 per cent of the costs for the latter. This is a much greater saving than that shown by the first estimates quoted above for which the equivalent saving was only 22 per cent. A third and earlier estimate (2) of the economies of scale for ironmaking, for which the conditions of a developed country were assumed, corresponded closely to the second set of estimates.

Steelmaking

There are several ways of making steel, which may involve any or all of the following three inputs, hot metal (iron), cold pig iron and scrap, in variable combinations. The economics of the various processes are to some extent determined by the relative prices of these inputs. In all the processes metal is charged into a furnace for melting and refining. When this process is complete the steel is usually poured from the furnace into a large ladle (commonly holding the whole of the furnace's output), from which it is 'teemed' into ingot moulds. There is a relatively small, although growing, amount of molten steel which is poured from the ladle, not into ingot moulds, but into 'continuous casting' machines which produce 'billets', 'blooms' or 'slabs' (thus dispensing with the need for a 'primary' mill, which reduces an ingot to a 'slab' or 'billet'). Continuous casting is dealt with separately below.

The proportions of steel made by each of the main methods used in the U.K. in 1957 and 1963 are shown below, together with estimates for 1970. The rapidly growing proportion accounted for by the new processes, such as the L-D process, will be noted.

---

(1) Economic Commission for Latin America, Inter-regional Symposium on the Application of Modern Technical Practices on the Iron and Steel Industry in Developing Countries (E.C.L.A. 1964), p. 28. This report described only the first results of research into the economies of scale in the steel industry obtained by E.C.L.A.

(2) United Nations. 'A study of the Iron and Steel Industry in Latin America' Vol. 1. New York 1954 (E.C.L.A. 1954), p. 113.

Table 4.1. Percentage of crude steel produced by types of process

	Open hearth	LD/Kaldo/ Rotor converters	Bessemer or other converters	Electric furnaces	Other processes
1957	87.7	—	6.0	5.6	0.7
1963	76.0	6.7	7.8	9.2	0.3
1970 (Estimated)	51.0	34.3	—	14.4	0.3

Source: Development in the Iron and Steel Industry Special Report, 1964.

We consider the economies of scale for each of the main types of furnace below.

1. Open-hearth furnaces

Although open-hearth furnaces are still the most common form of steel-making furnace in the U.K., no new furnaces of this type are being built. The process is very flexible in the metal/scrap ratio with which it can operate, but traditionally the process has quite a lengthy cycle time, about eight hours. This allows accurate and extensive metallurgical control of the steelmaking but presents problems because subsequent operations require a continuous flow of steel ingots.

There was a discussion of the factors affecting the choice of size of steel furnace in the Productivity Team Report(1) on the Iron and Steel Industry It was stated that all the main elements of cost fall as the size of a furnace increases, resulting in considerable economies of scale. Capital charges per ton of steel rise less than proportionately, labour charges vary little with size of furnace, and most overheads are, as usual, largely independent of the size of furnace. Fuel consumption rates,(2) refractory wear, and surface heat losses, all come down as size increases.

Some minor elements of furnace costs probably increase after a point more than proportionately with size. Crane capacity, and therefore cost, is often quoted as becoming a limitation on size of furnaces. In the past the main restriction to the size of open-hearth furnaces has been that rolling requires a fairly constant supply of ingots. If the ingots are supplied in very large and infrequent batches very great losses of heat are incurred, and heavy expenditure on additional soaking pits to keep the ingots at the correct temperature for rolling is required. After a point the cost of reheating would offset the savings from larger furnaces. This consideration sets a lower limit to the number of furnaces, and, there-

---

(1) Iron and Steel Productivity Team Report published by Anglo-American Council on Productivity, London, 1952, p.26.

(2) Iron and Steel, p.64.

fore, with any given total output sets an upper limit to the size of furnace. It is a consideration which is applicable only to cases where the cycle time for steelmaking is lengthy. Oxygen converters, with a cycle time which is less than one hour, are not subject to this constraint on their size if the steelmaking and rolling rates per hour are reasonably geared.

Some estimates were made in 1952 (1) in the United States of comparative capital investment costs for basic open-hearth melting shops of different annual capacities. These show how the capital cost per annual ton falls as the total size of the steelmaking plant increases. Four sizes of plant were considered; 100, 000, 250, 000, 500, 000, and 1, 000, 000 metric tons p.a. The total capital costs, per ton of annual capacity, including those for buildings, furnaces and auxiliaries, ancillary equipment, and services, but not including any provision for working capital, fall as the size of melting shop increases, as the following indices show

100, 000 tons p.a.	250, 000 tons p.a.	500, 000 tons p.a.	1, 000, 000 tons p.a.
124	100	81	74

These decreasing capital costs per ton are due partly to the larger furnaces in the larger plants, and partly to the less than proportionate rise in costs per ton for buildings and other equipment. The 100, 000 tons p.a. plant is taken as having two 65-ton furnaces, the 250, 000 ton p.a. plant as having three 118-ton furnaces, the 500, 000 ton p.a. plant as having four 182-ton furnaces, and the 1, 000, 000 ton p.a. plant as having seven 215-ton furnaces. Indices of the capital costs per ton of the furnaces alone are given below.

100, 000 tons p.a.	250, 000 tons p.a.	500, 000 tons p.a.	1, 000, 000 tons p.a.
123	100	71	70

Data supplied by the Iron and Steel Board show a relationship between the operating costs of producing steel in different sized open-hearth furnaces, all assumed to be in melting shops producing an annual output in the region of 0.5 to 0.75 million tons. The figures are based on the costs of actual plants, but have been adjusted to eliminate as far as possible the effects on costs of factors other than those directly or indirectly attributable to the size of the furnace. The figures are as follows:-

---

(1) (E.C.L.A. 1954), Vol. II, pp. 316-327. (See p. 67, n. 2).

Table 4.2. Operating costs and size for open-hearth furnaces

Size of furnaces (tons)	Index of operating costs per ton (excl. the cost of materials)
75	131
150	100
250	94
400	85

Some estimates of operating costs for melting shops of varying capacity with open-hearth furnaces were given in a recent study(1). These estimates showed that labour costs and, to a lesser extent, other operating costs such as maintenance decrease with scale. The following indices are for operating costs and illustrate these economies.

100,000 tons p.a.	200,000 tons p.a.	500,000 tons p.a.	1,000,000 tons p.a.	1,500,000 tons p.a.
106	100	79	74	71

Estimates of the capital costs per ton declined more rapidly than operating costs so that the total costs per ton excluding ferrous materials fall as follows:-

107	100	79	70	65

2. Electric-arc furnaces

Electric steelmaking is still responsible for only a small, although increasing, proportion of the total output of steel in the U.K., the U.S.A., and Europe. There are two kinds of electric furnaces, arc and induction furnaces, the former being used in processes for which a substantial amount of refining takes place. Arc furnaces also have great advantages for the production of steels containing a high proportion of alloys—'special steels'—since sensitive control of temperatures is possible and process losses of the expensive alloys are small. Most stainless steel, and high manganese and high silicon steels, are made in arc furnaces, which are also used for very high-quality steels from which it is important to exclude impurities.

A comparison has been made by a large steel company of the costs of producing steel from 100 per cent scrap by a single slag process in different-sized electric-arc furnaces operating a continuous working week.

(1) E.C.L.A. 1964 (see p. 67, n. 1).

The heat sizes compared range from 5 tons to 100 tons, and the estimate of capital and operating costs (the former based upon an annual 5 per cent depreciation charge and an annual return on capital of 15 per cent) fall as follows:

5 tons	10 tons	20 tons	40 tons	75 tons	100 tons
286	170	124	100	89	81

The recent study made by the Economic Commission for Latin America (E.C.L.A. 1964 p. 79 n. 1.) gave estimates for steel-melting shops of varying capacities using electric furnaces. These estimates showed similar economies for investment and operating costs to those shown for open-hearth furnaces. But the absolute operating costs, including capital charges, were estimated to be 14 per cent less than for the open-hearth furnace shop for 100, 000 ton size and some 12 per cent less for the 1, 500, 000 ton size.

3. Bessemer converters

Estimates were made in 1952 (1) of the capital costs of all equipment in and associated with (a) acid Bessemer and (b) basic Bessemer steel-making plants. Both Bessemer processes are limited in the amount of scrap which they can melt, and in order to use up all the mill scrap and maintain a scrap balance it was assumed in these estimates that some auxiliary electric furnaces were provided. The costs of these are included in the following figures. For the acid process, there were two 10-ton converters and one 17-ton electric furnace in the 100, 000 tons p.a. plant, for the 250, 000 tons p.a. plant two 15-ton converters and two 23-ton electric furnaces, and for the 500, 000 tons p.a. plant two 15-ton converters and two 43-ton electric furnaces. For the basic process the plant included was as follows:

100, 000 tons p.a.	250, 000 tons p.a.	500, 000 tons p.a.	1, 000, 000 tons p.a.
2-10 ton converters	3-11 ton converters	3-22 ton converters	3-44 ton converters
1-10 ton electric furnace	2-13 ton electric furnaces	2-26 ton electric furnaces	2-32 ton electric furnaces

The capital costs per ton were as follows, showing marked economies of scale,

tons p.a.	100, 000	250, 000	500, 000	1, 000, 000
Acid Bessemer	167	100	70	—
Basic Bessemer	162	100	68	54

(1) E.C.L.A. 1954. Vol. II pp. 316-327 (see p. 67. n. 2.)

No estimates of operating costs for melting shops of varying size using Bessemer Converters were given in this study. However, data given in a study of steelmaking processes (1) indicate that for production costs economies with Bessemer converters are slightly smaller than for melting shops with open-hearth furnaces.

4. Oxygen steelmaking

The term 'oxygen steelmaking' is given to those processes which involve the addition of oxygen during the steelmaking. They have become important during the last 10 years. It was the advent of cheap tonnage oxygen which enabled the advantages of the oxygen steelmaking processes—simplicity, relatively low capital costs and high production rates—to be obtained. They are now the basic and often the sole method of steelmaking in the new integrated works coming into operation, such as the Spencer Works at Newport of Richard Thomas and Baldwins, and the Dunkerque Works of the Société Dunkerqueoise de Sidérurgie.

One of these processes is the L-D process in which a blast of oxygen is directed from above onto the molten iron in the converter. The oxygen combines with the phosphorus, silicon and other elements in the iron to reduce it to steel in the comparatively short time of about 45-50 minutes. At the Spencer Works the output from three 100/120-ton converters, one of which is always out of production for relining, exceeds 1.75 million ingot tons per annum. Individual vessels with a capacity of up to 275 tons, giving an annual capacity of 2 million tons, are now being installed in other countries.

An engineering estimate of the capital costs of steelmaking plant using the L-D process, in one instance to produce an annual output of 100,000 tons, in the other 1,000,000 tons and assuming the conditions of an emergent country, shows the cost per ton to be £14.8 and £6.3 respectively. Estimated operating costs of steelmaking (excluding the cost of pig iron scrap and other materials) fell from £1.3 to £.85 respectively. Charging 5 per cent p.a. depreciation and 20 per cent for return on capital, the costs per ton of ingot steel (excluding materials) were estimated at £4.3 and £2.0 respectively.

In a comparison of the main steelmaking processes prepared by the Economic Commission for Europe, (2) and published in 1962, a comparison of relative investment costs per ton of steel was given. One set of data showed estimates of the investment costs for steel shops using the various processes that have been mentioned. This comparison showed marked economies of scale for each type of process. For all the processes, investment costs per ton for shops with an annual capacity of one million tons were estimated to be about 50 per cent of those for shops with less than 50,000 tons capacity. Investment costs were estimated

---

(1) Economic Commission for Europe. Comparison of steelmaking Processes (E.C.E. 1962), p. 68. New York 1962.

(2) E.C.E. 1962, p. 60.

to fall by approximately a further 15 per cent between one million tons and 1.8 million tons per annum. These comparisons are in line with those given earlier in this section.

For new steel-melting shops, oxygen converters and electric furnaces would be the most economical type of furnace, (1) and a choice between the two would be determined by relative fuel costs, relative costs of pig iron and scrap and by the type of products made. Both types of furnace have a relatively short cycle time, and the development of these furnaces has tended to reduce the number of furnaces in a melting shop. This is because it is no longer necessary to have a battery of furnaces to pro-vide rolling mills with steel at frequent intervals. At first these new types of furnace were of smaller capacity per heat than furnaces they replaced, but the maximum size of L-D furnaces in particular is increas-ing and these furnaces can now be built with a very high capacity per heat.

5. Continuous Casting

This new process is an alternative way of converting liquid steel from the furnace into a solid form suitable for further processing. The tradi-tional method is to tap the steel from the furnace into a bucket-shaped ladle, from which the liquid is poured into cast-iron moulds of various shapes and sizes. After solidification, the moulds are removed and the in-gots, usually fairly massive, are transferred to reheating furnaces where they 'soak' at temperatures which make them suitable for later hot work-ing operations, usually rolling, sometimes forging. There are several hot rolling operations which reduce the cross-sectional dimensions; these may involve intermediate heating in reheating furnaces.

The idea behind the new process is not a new one. Henry Bessemer tried in 1856 to produce a continuously poured thin strip or sheet from a pair of water-cooled rolls. In the modern process, the liquid steel is poured, from the ladle into which the furnace has been tapped, into the casting machine, which is so arranged that one or more rod-like streams of the metal discharge vertically downwards, into moulds of the section requir-ed, from which the solidified steel is continuously withdrawn. The metal is cooled quickly in these moulds, which are usually of high-grade metal, such as chromium-plated pure copper, which ensures excellent surface quality. Much trouble is caused in making ingot steel by the formation of impurities during solidification, but the high rate of solidification attained in continuous casting machines results in the virtual absence of such pockets of impurities.

---

(1) A discussion of costs for different processes is given in Chapter 5 of the Economic Commission for Europe's 'Comparison of Steel Making Processes'. One comparison of steelmaking shops with a capacity of a million tons gave the following index numbers of production costs for the main types of process discussed above: Open Hearth 100, Electric furnace 90.1. Bessemer Converter 93.3 L.D.—A.C.85.5.

The advantages of the process are:

1. High yield—the yield by continuous casting is in the region of 95 per cent compared to about 86 per cent for the same semi-finished product via a primary mill.

2. Semi-finished products are produced, thus eliminating the need for a primary mill.

3. Relatively low capital cost.

The way in which the total output of a continuous casting machine is determined by the size of the billet produced is shown by the following data. The figures are for one 'strand' only. A casting machine can have more than one strand, and six are considered at present to be the probable practicable limit. The advantage of having more than one strand in a machine is that the 'heat' (1) of steel does not have to be divided into two or more ladles, but there is not much difference in equipment, and therefore in capital cost, between a double-strand machine and two single-strand machines.

Billet size (inches X inches)	2"	2½"	3"	3½"	4"	4½"	5"	5½"	6"
Casting rate (tons per hour)	8	9	11	12	13	14	15	15	16

A limitation on the operation of continuous casting machines is the fact that steel will remain liquid in the ladle for about one hour only.

The size of billet is determined by the finished articles to be produced, and therefore there is little or no opportunity for increasing the output of the machine, and lowering average costs per ton, by increasing the size of mould, given any particular final product. Moreover, if the mould size is increased, the main savings are in labour costs, which are relatively insignificant. The annual capacity of a machine making 6" billets is approximately 120, 000 tons. The economies which can be achieved by the use of machines with more than one strand are small, so the economies of scale for continuous casting are relatively unimportant compared with those for other steelmaking processes. They are very much smaller than the economies of scale for the techniques of primary rolling which continuous casting replaces.

Finishing processes

It has not been possible to investigate the economies of scale for all the finishing processes used in the industry, and we have concentrated our study on rolling operations. Most of the information given in this section of the paper has been drawn from a paper by W. F. Cartwright and

---

(1) i.e. the contents of a batch from the steelmaking furnace.

M. F. Dowding, 'The Effect of Plant Design and Layout on Capital and Operating Costs'(1) published in January, 1958. In this paper a comparison was made for the four types of rolling plant, listed below. We also show the output range for each type of equipment.

Types of flat rolling plant

	Output ingot tons per year
1. Steckel hot strip mill and reversing cold mills	120,000-350,000
2. Semi-continuous hot strip mill and reversing cold mills	300,000-500,000
3. Semi-continuous hot strip mill and tandem cold mills	500,000-800,000
4. Continuous hot strip mill and tandem cold mills	1,250,000-2,500,000

To enable comparisons of costs to be made, it was assumed that four types of steel product were made, and capital and other operating costs were apportioned to the various products. The following table shows the estimated differences in costs, assuming each plant was operated at full capacity. Capital charges, man-hours, heat consumption, and total costs per ton of finished product all fall sharply as the scale of plant increases. Also the yield of finished product per slab of steel tends to rise with the scale of the plant.

Table 4.3. Costs and types of flat rolling plant

Plant	Plate	Hot rolled sheet	Cold rolled sheet	Tinplate
Capital investment per annual ton of prime product				
	£			
1	65	61.5	85.0	130
2	43.8	52.8	84.0	117
3	33.3	39.3	53.0	86
4	15.4	16.4	30.0	43.5

(1) J. Iron St. Inst., January, 1958.

Table 4.3. Costs and types of flat rolling plant-contd

Plant	Plate	Hot rolled sheet	Cold rolled sheet	Tinplate
Capital charge per ton at 9 per cent per annum				
	£			
1	5.85	5.54	7.65	11.7
2	3.94	4.75	7.56	10.5
3	3.0	3.54	4.77	7.7
4	1.38	1.49	2.70	3.9
Man hours per ton of finished product				
1	3.5	2.4	4.0	5.3
2	2.4	1.2	2.4	3.7
3	2.1	1.0	1.8	2.9
4	0.6	0.7	1.2	2.1
Heat consumption per ton of finished product—10^6 B.T.U.				
1	3.1	3.2	5.2	5.0
2	2.8	2.7	4.4	4.4
3	2.8	2.7	3.9	4.3
4	2.3	2.4	3.5	3.6
Operating cost per ton of prime product				
	£			
1	8.5	8.5	17.1	22.0
2	8.3	7.2	13.9	19.5
3	8.0	7.0	11.0	16.5
4	5.5	6.2	10.0	13.3
Total operating costs per ton including capital charges				
	£			
(Figures in brackets are an index of cost per ton with the cost per ton for the smallest plant taken as 100)				
1	14.3 (100)	14.0 (100)	24.7 (100)	33.7 (100)
2	12.2 (85)	11.9 (85)	21.5 (87)	30.0 (89)
3	11.0 (77)	10.5 (75)	15.8 (64)	24.2 (72)
4	6.9 (48)	7.7 (55)	12.7 (51)	17.2 (51)

The economies of the larger plants are marked, and the total costs per ton for the smallest scale of plant are approximately twice that for the largest size. It has not been possible to obtain estimates for the economies of scale for continuous hot strip mills with levels of capacity other than that shown, but it is understood that there are marked economies of scale over the range of 1 million to 3 million tons per annum, and economies continue even beyond this. There is one qualification to these estimates. The larger plants are less flexible. Where small orders for special gauges and sizes of steel are required, the large-scale continuous mills are at a disadvantage because of the potential production lost while the plant is adjusted.

An estimate (1) made in 1952, for which the conditions of a developed country were assumed, also indicated that the economies of scale were greater for rolling operations than for iron and steel conversion. For this exercise it was assumed that the product mix of plants was not affected by their output. The estimated economies in capital costs are smaller than those indicated by the previous data. Nevertheless, the overall economies shown are substantial.

Table 4.4. Rolling costs per ton for plants of sizes located at Sparrows Point, U.S.A., in 1952

(Costs for plant with a capacity of 250,000 tons p.a. = 100)

	Output—tons per annum			
	50,000	250,000	500,000	1,000,000
Labour	191	100	51	36
Overheads and Power	200	100	100	100
Capital Charges	127	100	93	90
Total (excluding cost of ingots)	172	100	73	64

The costs of handling materials (2)

The costs of handling materials are an important element in the costs of a steelworks, and it has been estimated that 35 per cent of the capital cost of a steelworks can be attributed to providing handling facilities. Four methods of handling the raw materials required in an iron and steelworks are road, rail, ropeway, and conveyor belt. The costs of carrying materials by these methods over varying distances with vary-

(1) E.C.L.A., 1954, Vol. 1., p. 116 (see p. 67, n. 2.)

(2) This section is based on a paper by P.M. Worthington on the 'Economies of Handling Materials in the Iron and Steel Industry', J. Iron St. Inst., October, 1962, p. 849.

ing levels of throughput have been calculated. All the methods exhibit economies of scale and these are illustrated by the figures given below for hauls of six miles. The costs include all operating costs, plus a 20 per cent return on capital employed, excluding the cost of land.

Table 4.5. Costs per ton to haul granular materials 6 miles (pence)

	Rail	Road	Ropeway	Conveyor
50 tons per hour	67	54	38	Extremely high
100 tons per hour	35	36	30	Very high
200 tons per hour	20	27	24	36
500 tons per hour	9	21	20	20
1,000 tons per hour	5	18	19	13

As the capacity of a steelworks grows this will marginally increase the length of hauls for raw materials. This is slightly offset by the tendency for the costs of haulage per ton mile to fall as the length of haul rises, but the extent to which economies of scale apply for this dimension depend on the method used. The data below illustrate these relationships.

Table 4.6. Costs per ton mile to haul 500 tons of granular material per hour over various distances (pence)

Length of haul (miles)	Rail	Road	Ropeway	Conveyor
2	3	$4\frac{1}{2}$	$4\frac{1}{2}$	$3\frac{1}{2}$
4	2	$3\frac{3}{4}$	$3\frac{3}{4}$	$3\frac{1}{2}$
6	$1\frac{1}{2}$	$3\frac{1}{2}$	$3\frac{1}{2}$	$3\frac{1}{2}$

Integrated steel plants

In addition to the processes already discussed separately, an integrated steelworks has coke ovens, sintering, oxygen making and other specialist plant. Estimates obtained from an engineering consultant show that there are marked economies of scale for sintering plant, and a recently published study indicates that there are also substantial economies for oxygen-making plant.[1] The economies of scale for cokemaking are thought to be less important. Since it is possible to buy out coke there is a floor to any diseconomies of scale in this department.

---

(1) E.C.E. 1962 (see p. 72, n. 1.) p. 10.

The particular economies of an integrated works, compared to specialist works for, say, finishing, are the savings in costs of reheating, the reduction of transport costs, particularly for scrap which is reused, and the possibility of co-ordinating the operations of the departments of the steelworks. The use of computers in place of the former 'rule of thumb' methods has increased the importance of the last-mentioned advantage of integrated works. Because of these economies of integrated steelworks, the steelworks which have been built on new sites in the U.K. since the war have all been integrated plants. Nevertheless, many specialist works still operate in this country. It is not possible to give a precise estimate of the diseconomies of separate works, because these will depend on the distances involved and the finishing operations performed. One reason for the viability of specialist works is that the diseconomies of separate works are often less than the extra costs involved in replacing them while their plant is still in good condition.

Table 4.7. gives an approximate breakdown of costs for an integrated steel company. This is derived from published company accounts and confidential information obtained from companies.

Table 4.7. A cost breakdown for an integrated steel company

	Percentage
Purchased materials	23
Fuel and Power	25
Wages, Salaries, and National Insurance	22
Manufacturing and general expenses	9
Delivery charges	7
Capital charges (15 per cent on capital)	14
	100

Table 4.8. shows the effect on costs of working below full capacity. The figures refer to a new integrated works making heavy steel products. As we should expect, unit costs rise fairly rapidly as the rate of working declines, because few economies can be made in labour and overhead costs as output declines and total capital charges are hardly affected by the level of working. The main savings achieved when the level of working declines are raw material and fuel costs.

We have attempted to make an overall estimate of the economies of scale for steelmaking. These estimates are primarily based on the data given in the preceding sections of the paper, but we have also used additional information obtained from companies. It is assumed that the finishing operations consist of rolling, and that the range of products includes sheet steel and is not affected by the total output, i.e. that to achieve greater output the plant does not have to diversify its production. Allowance has been made for economies in raw materials and fuel, since

Table 4.8. Short-run costs and the level
of capacity working

Level of working	Index of unit costs (costs at full capacity = 100)
%	
100	100
95	$101\frac{1}{2}$
90	104
85	107
80	110
75	113

economies could be achieved in their transport and processing and in the
efficiency with which they are used. Our estimates of the overall economies of scale are shown below.

Table 4.9. Production costs and scale (1)

(Unit costs per ton for a plant with a capacity of 250,000 tons = 100)

	Output—000 tons per annum					
	100	250	500	1,000	2,000	4,000
Blast furnaces	120	100	94	89	85	82
Steel furnaces	125	100	90	82	78	75
Finishing	137	100	82	68	56	47
Total	128	100	89	79	72	67

(1) Raw material costs are included at the stage of steelmaking when
they are introduced, e.g. iron ore is included as a cost for blast furnaces and steel scrap as a cost of steel furnaces, but the costs exclude the cost of materials transferred from the preceding process,
e.g. the costs for steel furnaces exclude the costs of pig iron.

These estimates give an indication of the economies of scale for an integrated works using oxygen converters and producing rolled products.
The extent of the economies of scale clearly depend on the type of finishing processes used. If a wide hot strip mill is included a capacity of at
least 3 million tons (10 per cent of total U.K. steel production capacity

and more than half the total U.K. output of sheet steel) is required in order to utilise the full potential of the most modern and efficient equipment. The maximum output of other types of rolling mill is much lower: for plate mills it is about a million tons. But a steelworks with a capacity of a million tons would not be the optimum size for a works producing plate. As we have seen, economies of scale for blast furnaces and melting shop continue beyond this level, and there would be advantages to be obtained by the duplication of rolling mills to provide flexibility, and to make it possible to extend production runs.

In 1952 J.S. Bain(1) estimated that the optimum size for an integrated steel mill ranged from 1 to $2\frac{1}{2}$ million tons per annum. In replies to a questionnaire he circulated it was suggested that unit costs might be up by as much as 5 per cent at 500,000 tons capacity. We have been convinced by our study of the industry that, in general, economies over the range taken by Bain are now greater than this, and that for some types of works economies of scale continue beyond $2\frac{1}{2}$ million tons. This increase in the optimum size of works has been caused by technical advances which have involved, inter alia, an increase in the size of units of plant. As we have seen, however, some technical developments, e.g. the reduction of furnace cycle times, and the development of continuous casting, have at least initially tended to reduce the optimum scale.

The structure of the industry, and conclusions

In 1963/64 nine companies with an output of more than a million tons capacity produced 78 per cent of the U.K. output of crude steel; the largest nineteen companies produced 94 per cent. Many of these companies operated more than one works, so these figures give a misleading impression of the degree of concentration in the industry. Of the 310 works producing steel products only eight had a capacity of more than a million tons a year, and these produced only 40 per cent of the common steel made in the U.K.

An indication of the diffusion of the industry is provided by the following data for blast furnaces.

Table 4.10. The size of blast furnaces

	1955	1962
Total number of blast furnaces	138	105
Average number of blast furnaces in blast	99	73
Average output per furnace per annum (000 tons)	126	187
Number of separate works with blast furnaces	47	38

Source: Iron and Steel Annual Statistics

(1) J.S. Bain, Barriers to New Competition, Cambridge, Mass. 1956.

Clearly some concentration of blast-furnace capacity has been achieved, both by the use of larger blast furnaces and by concentration on fewer works. But the scope for further concentration of output is illustrated by the fact that the total U.K. output of pig iron could be produced in 20 of the largest blast furnaces now being built. Similarly, it could be shown that in terms of up-to-date equipment the average size of steel furnaces and finishing plant used by the British steel industry is below the optimum size. There is also some evidence to show that U.K. companies are operating on a smaller scale, both in terms of the output of companies and of works, than some of their overseas competitors, notably in the United States, Western Germany, Russia, and Japan.

Our estimates of the economies of scale for the industry have been based on the assumption that the output of a works does not affect the range of products made. In practice, the scale on which particular products are made is limited by the absolute size of the market and by competitors. Small works making products for which specialist plant is required, and for which finishing costs are relatively important, can remain competitive in spite of economies of scale, especially if their capital equipment has been heavily written down. However, even allowing for this, the structure of the U.K. steel industry seems to consist of too many small units for optimum efficiency. Some of these works can, no doubt, be justified on the grounds that they make specialist products or that they use plant which has not yet reached the end of its useful life, but it is very unlikely that all of them can be justified on these grounds. A detailed investigation of the economic and social consequences would, however, be needed before firm conclusions could be drawn about any desirable reorganisation of the industry.

A feature of our study of economies of scale in the steel industry is that many of the estimates of these economies which we have obtained show no sign of costs ceasing to fall with scale even though the rate at which they fall declines. If works were constructed to produce, say, 20 million tons of steel a year, there is no clear technical reason to doubt that yet larger scale plant would be designed, and that there would be some economies of scale up to this level of output, provided the range of products was not affected by the level of output.

5 Oil Refining

Introduction

The consumption of petroleum products in the United Kingdom increased from 8. 8 to 47. 2 million tons between 1938 and 1962, and by 1962 oil accounted for 29 per cent (1) of the total consumption of primary fuels. During the same period, the throughput of crude oil of U.K. refineries increased from $2\frac{1}{2}$ million to 47 million tons. In terms of employees the oil-refining industry is still relatively unimportant—the 20, 000 people employed in the industry represent less than one tenth of one per cent of the total working population—but in terms of the value of output, or of capital employed, the industry ranks among the largest manufacturing industries.

The oil-refining industry was selected for this study of the economies of large-scale production because it is a large-scale, capital-intensive industry, because we expected that there would be reliable estimates of the relationship between unit costs and size of refinery, and because the industry has invested heavily in recent years and there are plans to expand U.K. refinery capacity rapidly. In addition, oil refining is typical of other important process chemical industries.

In this chapter we first outline the processes and equipment employed by the industry. We then discuss the factors which an oil company considers in planning a new refinery, so that the importance of technical economies of scale can be seen in perspective. In the next section of the chapter, estimates of the costs of refining are given as a basis for estimating the economies of scale, which are considered in the following section. Finally, we view our estimates of the economies of scale in relation to the existing structure of the industry.

Processes

Crude oil is a mixture of substances which are formed of two elements, carbon and hydrogen, with the addition of some impurities, of which sulphur is the most important. The atoms of hydrogen and carbon combine in a large number of distinct 'hydrocarbon' molecules, and the structure of these 'hydrocarbons' determines the properties of the oil. The purpose of refining is to break down the crude oil, which includes different types of 'hydrocarbons', so that the properties of each 'cut' are consistent and conform to the market requirements.

The structure of the 'hydrocarbons' determines their boiling point and this makes it possible to split up the crude oil by distillation, the fundamental refining process. Another method of splitting the crude is the use of solvents to separate those constituents of the crude which have

---

(1) Measured in terms of coal equivalent. Source-Ministry of Power Statistical Digest, 1963.

the same or similar boiling points and differing properties, for example to remove asphalt from lubricating oil, or to extract elements such as sulphur.

The products of the distillation process may not meet the requirements of the pattern of market demand because the product yield required cannot be obtained from the crude oil available. Some flexibility is provided by the fact that the composition of crude oil varies according to its source. For example, Libyan crude contains a higher proportion of light distillate than Kuwait crude, and Kuwait crude contains more heavy fuel oil. The major oil companies may draw the crude which they refine in the U.K. from more than one source, and they can to some extent control the flow of crude to meet the pattern of the market demand. This flexibility is however insufficient, and thermal and catalytic 'cracking', and other processes for reforming the structure of the oil, are employed. These processes were first introduced in the U.S.A. for breaking down heavy oils with a high boiling point into lighter components for inclusion in motor spirit blends, for which demand is proportionately much greater in the U.S.A. than in Europe, and for which the return is very much higher than for some heavy oil products such as fuel oil.

Many additional processes are used in a modern refinery to provide flexibility and to ensure that refined products have the required market quality e.g. colour, odour, stability etc. A large-scale refinery produces hundreds of types and grades of product and may have as many as twenty separate major process units.

The capacity of a refinery is usually measured in terms of its distillation capacity, and for a consideration of the economies of scale distillation units are of some importance, because after this stage of processing the oil is broken down into its main components of light, middle and heavy distillates and the subsequent processes therefore deal with smaller individual streams of oil. A distillation process unit essentially consists of a pipestill and a distillation column. A pipestill is a brick built, oil- or gas-fired furnace, through which oil is pumped in tubes. After being heated in a pipestill the oil enters the base of the distillation column in part liquid, part vapour, form. The pressure in the column varies so that the gas condenses as it rises up the column. Five main 'cuts' are usually made in the distillation column, from which the oil is piped away for further treatment or processing.

In what follows we have not considered the economies of scale for the other process units individually. Most of these processes are carried out under high pressure and temperature in pressure vessels, and a large-scale refinery may contain many such units. The shells of the pressure vessels are usually made of high-grade steel, the type of which is determined by the function of the vessel. The units may weigh as much as 450 tons, with dimensions up to 150 feet in height and 26 feet in diameter.

When a new refinery is built, other items of capital equipment in addition to process units are required. These may include jetties for unloading and loading tankers, roads, a fire station, laboratories and offices, power and steam generating equipment, storage tanks and equipment for disposing of waste products. In practice the cost of this 'offsite' equipment and the cost of preparing the site represent an important part of the total cost of building a refinery.

As was mentioned earlier, the labour force employed in a refinery is quite small relative to the capital employed. The new Esso refinery at Milford Haven with a capacity of nearly 5 million tons per annum, which cost about £18 million to build, is operated by about 330 employees. The labour force required depends on the range of processes used and on the type of products made. If some products have to be packaged in small lots, e.g. cans of lubricating oil, this can be an important factor creating a demand for labour. The varying extent to which work such as maintenance is sub-contracted is another factor which invalidates comparisons between refineries in terms of the number of tons of capacity per employee.

Automation has probably been carried further in this industry than in any other, and the rate of flow of oil, its temperature, quality and composition are continuously measured and regulated by instruments. The processes are automated to such an extent that the staff required for maintenance and cleaning of a new refinery is usually larger than that required for operating the process equipment. From time to time items of equipment have to be shut down and overhauled, though the periods between major overhauls have been greatly extended, and for many refineries the overhaul and maintenance work is sub-contracted.

Planning a new refinery

Over 95 per cent of the oil refinery capacity in the U.K. is controlled by integrated oil companies which also prospect and drill for oil overseas, produce and control its shipment to the U.K. and its refining and distribution. Such companies plan their operations on a world-wide scale, and their first consideration in planning new refinery capacity is the expected growth in total demand for oil products, and the market share that they can hope to obtain. An oil company is reluctant to build refineries far in advance of demand, because the capital used will be temporarily unproductive and because future technical developments may reduce refinery capital and operating costs.

Oil companies would ideally site new refinery capacity to meet the demand for their product at the lowest cost, but in practice political pressures influence their decisions. During the early post-war period, European governments pressed the oil companies to build refineries in Europe to reduce the foreign exchange cost of importing finished products, and the many new refineries which have been built in Europe are partly the result of this pressure. The governments of many developing countries are now applying similar pressure and some small-scale refineries have recently been built, and more may be expected to be built, in response to these demands.

The third factor determining the site of new refinery capacity is the total cost of transport. After the cost of producing the crude, transport costs of crude and refined oil are the largest single element in the costs of refined oil, and they exceed the cost of refining operations. The costs of transport depend on the possibility of using sea transport and pipe-lines to deliver crude oil, the area covered by markets, and the methods available for the delivery of products. It is, however, impossible to quantify the relationship between scale of refinery and transport costs except by reference to particular circumstances.

When planning new refinery capacity a choice will have to be made between extending existing refineries or building completely new ones, and it may sometimes be more economic to extend an existing refinery in circumstances, where, if the company were starting from scratch, it would build two refineries. The possibility of exporting some of the products of a refinery is, however, a useful source of flexibility for a company faced with a decision of this type. It may be able to export surplus products to other markets, until the market of the country in which the refinery is to be situated has expanded sufficiently to take up its full capacity. Another possibility is the construction of a refinery as a joint venture by two or more companies.

If it is decided to build a new refinery, a decision has to be taken on the process units to include i.e. whether the new refinery is to make a complete or a partial range of products. The decision on the complexity of a refinery affects not only the product range. It also has important consequences for the flexibility of a refinery: the extent to which it can vary its product mix. This is an important requirement because of changes in the pattern of demand for refined products—for example, during a severe winter the demand for fuel oil may rise and that for motor spirit fall. The effect of the decision on operating costs is illustrated by the estimates shown in table 5.1. The inclusion of a catalytic cracking process increases operating costs per ton of throughput by nearly 50 per cent. An increase in the complexity of a refinery can however be expected to increase revenue because the average price for the product mix will be increased, or because the ability to supply a full

Table 5.1. Relative refinery operating costs as affected by the complexity of a refinery.

Type of refinery	Relative cost to process one ton
(a) Crude still, plus catalytic reforming	100
(b) (a) plus hydro-desulphurising of gas oil	113
(c) (b) plus bitumen plant	116
(d) (c) plus catalytic cracking	172

Source: 'New technology helps reduce the costs of smaller refineries.' World Petroleum April 1963   The data were prepared by K. L. Hagemans and R. E. Ingall.

range of products and to meet seasonal fluctuations in demand will give a competitive advantage. (1)

We shall show later in this chapter that there are considerable economies associated with large-scale refining, but this is only one of the factors an oil company takes into account when planning a new refinery. We have described some of the other factors to put the significance of economies of scale into perspective. The fact that there are these other important factors determining the size of refineries means that we cannot assume that the size of refineries actually built reflects the optimum long-run costs of refining. It also means that, because of the striking effect of variations in the cost of refining associated with variations in complexity, comparisons of costs per ton of throughput for actual refineries with different levels of capacity are particularly difficult to make.

Cost analysis

In this section we describe the costs of operating a new refinery with about 5 million tons per annum of capacity. It is assumed that the refinery produces a range of products in proportion to the total output of U.K. refineries. Table 5.2 shows our approximate estimates of the opera-

Table 5.2. Operating costs for a refinery with a capacity of 5 million tons(1)

	Per ton of finished products		Percentage of total costs
	s.	d.	
Process pay roll and supervision	2	0	7
Maintenance—Labour and materials	4	6	15
Utilities and Fuel	6	0	20
Catalysts and Chemicals	4	0	13
Depreciation	7	6	25
Other	6	0	20
	30	0	100

(1) The cost of the crude oil is excluded.

---

(1) For a discussion and an illustration of the effect of the inclusion of various process units on the product mix and product flexibility see The Growth of Integrated Oil Companies by J. G. Maclean and R. W. Haigh, p. 567, et seq.

ting costs of such a refinery. It has not been possible to obtain actual operating cost data for refineries, but the question of costs has been discussed with oil company accountants and the estimates shown in table 5. 2 are based on these discussions, and on published information in the Ministry of Power Statistical Digest, oil trade journals and company accounts.

For the purpose of estimating these costs it was assumed that the refinery operates at 100 per cent of normal capacity. The charge for utilities and fuel includes gas and oil used as refinery fuel. U.K. refineries consumed 3. 6 million tons of gas and oil as refinery fuel in 1962, or 7 per cent of crude throughput. It is difficult to price this fuel because some of the oil and gas used tends to be of residual types which it would be difficult to place in other markets. The charge assumed for depreciation is 7 per cent of investment costs, this charge being an average rate for process plant and 'offsite' equipment and a measure of wear and tear and obsolescence, which vary considerably for different items of equipment. Offices and jetties may last indefinitely, but the rapid technical development of processes and process equipment means that process units have to be written off by a depreciation charge of about 10 per cent per year. 'Other costs' include packaging materials, royalties, research expenditure, insurance and local taxation etc.

So far the only measure of the capital input used in estimating the cost of refinery operations has been the depreciation charge. Clearly a further allowance must be included for interest on capital employed. If a rate of 7 per cent on fixed capital is used this would be the same as the depreciation charge and the total costs of refining would then amount to 37s. 6d. per ton, excluding any allowance for interest on working capital.

The approximate average cost of the crude imported into the U.K. in 1963 was £7 a ton. Thus the cost of refining, 37s. 6d., represents on average about 20 per cent of the ex-refinery cost of refined products (£8 17s. 6d.). The ex-refinery price of products, excluding excise duties, varied in 1963 between about £6 per ton for fuel oil and more than £20 per ton for lubricating oils—the average net ex-refinery price was probably about £9 per ton of crude processed. These figures are intended to give an indication only of the order of magnitude of costs and revenue, and the difference between average revenue and costs of 2s. 6d. per ton is not a reliable guide to profits on refining. In view of the fact that more than 95 per cent of refinery capacity in the U.K. is owned by integrated oil companies there is no unambiguous price for crude, so that it is not possible to calculate the profit of these oil companies for any particular operation such as oil refining except on some arbitrary basis. Their profits are attributable to the whole spectrum of operations from exploration to delivery.

Table 5. 3 shows an estimate of the effect on refinery unit operating costs of idle capacity. As we should expect, unit operating costs rise rapidly as the level of capacity utilisation falls. The reductions in operating costs which can be made are small and are limited in the main to the costs of utilities, fuel and chemicals. It will be shown below that there are economies of scale for large refineries and that these economies are greater for fixed costs than for utilities, fuel and chemical costs. It follows that the effect of idle capacity on the unit operating costs of a small refinery is greater than for larger refineries.

Table 5.3. The effect of idle capacity on unit operating costs

Percentage of capacity idle	Relative costs to process one ton of crude
nil	100
10	109
20	118
30	129

Source: 'New Technology Helps Reduce Costs of Smaller Refineries'. World Petroleum, April 1963. The data were prepared by K. L. Hagemans and R. E. Ingall.

Economies of scale in oil refining

We have already shown the effects of the complexity of a refinery on its operating costs and mentioned the impact of technical development on labour requirements. There are only 17 refineries operating in the U.K. A comparison of the costs of refining per ton for these refineries, even if obtainable, would not give us a satisfactory guide to the economies of scale in the industry. This is because of the small numbers involved and the differences in age and complexity of the refineries. For our estimates of the economies of scale in this industry we have therefore relied mainly on 'engineering' estimates of capital and operating costs of refineries of varying size.

The most obvious economies of scale in refining are associated with plant costs. As we have seen, plant costs can be divided between process and offsite costs. In the U.S.A. it has been found that the costs of offsite investment are, on the average, 43 per cent of process equipment costs. (1) Clearly this relationship must depend on the site of the refinery, whether jetties have to be built, the complexity of the refinery etc. In the case of one large-scale U.K. refinery the cost of offsite investment, including site preparation, represented three-quarters of the total initial investment costs, partly because offsite facilities in excess of immediate requirements were installed.

It was from a study of the relationship between process plant costs and plant size, for equipment used in the petroleum and other process indu-

---

(1) W. L. Nelson. 'Oil and Gas Journal', 29th May 1963.

stries, that the so-called 0.6 rule for plant costs was first suggested. The 0.6 rule states that if capacity is measured in Y units and the cost of process plant in X units, then the relationship between capital cost and capacity for two units will be $\dfrac{X_1}{X_2} = \dfrac{Y_1}{Y_2}^{0.6}$ i.e. if the capacity of a plant is doubled then the capital cost is increased to $2^{0.6}$ i.e. by 52 per cent. The rule was based on the cost and capacity of individual units of plant, such as distillation units. Empirical work (1) based on the price of plant has shown that an approximate relationship of this kind exists, though the calculated factor for different kinds of plant varies between 0.5 and 0.9. The estimates relate to the range of plant sizes in production and cannot be assumed to extend beyond it. The process manager of a construction company, with whom we discussed the 0.6 rule, confirmed that the factors applied over the middle of the range of sizes produced, and that economies tend to be greater than those implied at the lower end and less towards the upper end, of the range of sizes made.

The 0.6 rule is attributable to the economies of large dimensions. The volume of pipes, tanks and pressure vessels determines their capacity, and the surface area determines steel requirements. If the gauge of steel is not affected, then volume and surface area are related in a similar way to the 0.6 rule. The gauge of steel required is in fact to some extent affected by size, but there are economies in the cost of steel because the gauge does not increase proportionately. Also the number of separate parts, which is an important determinant of the cost of fabrication, does not increase in proportion to scale for many items of process equipment such as tanks and pumps.

The distillation unit is the piece of equipment through which all the crude has to pass, and the largest of these units now in service has a capacity of about 10 million tons a year. Though technical economies of scale of capital costs apply for these units up to this level, it is argued that at levels of refinery output below this level it may be worth having more than one smaller unit to provide flexibility—for example to make it possible to take a unit out of service for maintenance without disrupting the whole refinery, and to make it possible to run two sorts of crude at the same time. The main reason for the present maximum size of these units would seem to be that nobody has so far built larger ones. There are apparently no insuperable technical reasons for stopping at this level but the first breakthrough carries some risks. Once the hurdle of obtaining experience of constructing larger units has been overcome, there will be economies of scale to be obtained by using larger units.

The data shown below, which were provided by a company operating in the U.K., illustrate the relationship between cost and output capacity for distillation units. For these estimates investment costs were based on the 0.6 rule and a charge for depreciation and return on capital amount-

---

(1) C. H. Chilton, ed. Cost Engineering in the Process Industries. New York 1960, and John Haldi, Economies of Scale in Economic Development. Department of Economics, Stanford University, Stanford, California, 1960.

ing to 13.6 per cent p.a. was assumed. The estimates of other operating costs, labour, supervision, maintenance and overheads were based on a comparison of costs of actual units of various sizes. As can be seen, the rate at which costs fall declines, but nevertheless a doubling of capacity from 5 to 10 million tons (the highest output considered) reduces costs per ton by 13 per cent.

Table 5.4. Operating costs per ton and scale for distillation units

Throughput capacity per year mn. tons	Index of operating costs per ton (excluding capital costs and crude oil)	Index of operating costs per ton excluding crude oil and including capital costs
1	100	100
2	77	67
5	63	51
10	55	44

Many of the items of process equipment, apart from the distillation unit, are to some extent optional, and whether particular items are installed depends on the range of products sold and the possibility of meeting special requirements from other refineries, as well as the throughput of the refinery itself. Thus the level of capacity at which it is necessary to duplicate these other process units varies. However, a representative of a construction company suggested that it would now be possible to build a typical refinery of 10 million tons capacity without duplicating any major process units. Above this level, the distillation unit would have to be duplicated but this would not apply to some of the other units.

J. G. Maclean and R. W. Haigh in 'The Growth of Integrated Oil Companies' describe a detailed study of the relationship between the size of refineries, as measured by their throughput, and their capital and operating costs. Their study was based upon an analysis made by a large company to determine the optimum size of refinery to build on the Gulf Coast of the U.S.A. in 1950. Capital and operating costs were estimated for five sizes of refinery with capital ranging from 0.5 to 10 million tons a year. The capital costs are shown in table 5.5. For the smaller refineries, these were estimated on the basis that these refineries would, with some minor adjustments, be scaled-down versions of the refinery of 10 million tons capacity. This is an unrealistic assumption, as it would not usually be economic to use the same processes, and these data therefore exaggerate the economies of scale.

The estimated variation in process plant investment costs with scale is shown in the first row of table 5.5. Over the range from 0.5 million tons to 3 million tons, unit process investment costs fall in line with the 0.6 rule. As capacity increases the rate of decline diminishes, as we should expect, and for a doubling of capacity from 5 million to 10 million tons costs fall by 10 per cent only.

Table 5.5. Investment for prime fuel products refineries at a Gulf Coast location in 1950

Refinery Size (million tons)	0.5	1.5	3.0	5.0	10.0
Investment –	(Cost per ton for a refinery with a capacity of 0.5 million tons = 100				
1. Process Equipment	100	66	52	45	41
2. Utilities, offsites, tankage and docks	100	63	53	48	43
3. Total Investment	100	64	53	47	42
4. 0.6 factor	100	63	48	39	29

Source: Based on Table 7, p. 46 of <u>Competition in Oil</u> by D. C. Hamilton. This table was derived from <u>The Growth of Integrated Oil Companies'</u> by J. G. Maclean and R. W. Haigh.

It is more difficult to generalise about the economies of scale of offsite equipment. For example, all the U.K. refineries are sited on or near the coast, and one major item of offsite capital equipment is the provision of jetties. It may be necessary to dredge a channel for tankers, and the site may impose a limit on the size of refinery by making it difficult to accommodate more than a certain number of tankers in a river entrance. Economies of scale apply to such items as roads, offices, jetties and electrical and steam generating plant, and from the Maclean and Haigh data shown in table 5.5 it is clear that these economies are substantial. The estimate in the table of the decline in unit offsite investment costs is very similar to that for process equipment.

Estimates of the relationship between capital costs and size for refineries built in the U.K. are shown in table 5.6. These estimates were made in 1958 by one of the companies operating in this country. For this exercise it was again assumed that the smaller refineries were scaled-down versions of the larger refineries. The estimates show economies of scale of approximately the same magnitude as shown by the earlier U.S. study. The main distinction between the two sets of estimates is

Table 5.6. Investment costs and scale for refineries built in the U.K. in 1958

Crude input mn. tons	Total investment costs per ton as a percentage of the costs of a refinery with a capacity of 1 mn. tons p.a.	0.6 factor
1	100	100
2	84	76
5	65	53
10	55	40

that the decline in costs is more marked over the higher range of output in the U.K. estimates.

So far we have considered the relationship between investment costs and scale for refineries. Now we introduce operating costs into the discussion. The main operating costs (which exclude crude oil) are direct labour, maintenance, utilities, fuel, chemicals and overheads. The number of personnel required to operate larger units increases slowly, even more slowly than investment costs. Maintenance costs are usually estimated to be a function of investment costs, and thus provide substantial economies of scale. Oil company accountants and engineers have assured us that the costs of on-site management of a refinery are small and that they are little affected by the size of refinery. Also there are economies for other overhead costs. The economies of one item of overheads, capital costs, have already been demonstrated. On the other hand, the cost of chemicals and fuel show relatively slight economies.

Estimates of the relationship between total operating costs and scale for Gulf Coast Refineries made by Maclean and Haigh are shown below. The index of operating costs, including depreciation, shows that costs at first fall rapidly as scale is increased but that the rate of fall diminishes as the capacity of refineries increases.

Operating costs and scale for refineries operating at 100 per cent of capacity

Scale – million tons	0.5	1.5	3.0	5.0	10.0
Index of total operating costs per ton	100	57	46	40	36

Table 5.7 gives some estimates of operating costs which were made at the same time as the study of capital costs of refineries built in the U.K. mentioned above. Column 2 shows the estimated operating costs, excluding depreciation, for refineries of differing sizes. These estimates exaggerate the economies of scale because the cost of works fuel is excluded. Any economies of scale for works fuel requirements are relatively insignificant. Depreciation estimated at $7\frac{1}{2}$ per cent of the capital cost of equipment is shown in column 3. A comparison of columns 2 and 3 indicates that economies of scale for operating and capital costs are of the same order of magnitude. Again the fall in costs over the range 5 to 10 million tons is greater than that given by the Maclean and Haigh study.

Another estimate of the economies of scale of operating costs of large refineries was reported in the article in the April 1963 issue of World Petroleum, 'New Technology Helps Reduce Costs of Smaller Refineries' and is shown in table 5.8. The estimated economies of scale are even more marked than those shown in table 5.7. The difference between the estimates is partly attributable to the fact that the estimates were made at different times, partly to differences in specification for the refineries, and partly to differences in the composition of costs (e.g.

Table 5.7. Refinery operating costs per ton and scale: I (1958)

Crude input capacity	Operating costs (excl. works fuel)	Depreciation	Total	0.6 factor
(Costs for refinery with a capacity of 1 mn. tons = 100)				
(1)	(2)	(3)	(4)	(5)
1	100	100	100	100
2	86	84	85	76
5	66	65	66	53
10	52	55	52	40

the operating costs shown in table 5.7 exclude works fuel). Apart from these factors there is inevitably an element of uncertainty about estimates of this sort.

Table 5.8. Refinery operating costs and scale: II (1963)

(Basis-simple refineries. without secondary processing, and operating at full capacity)

Input capacity (mn. tons)	Relative costs to process barrel of crude
0.5	100
1.0	71
2.0	54
4.0	44

Some of the estimates of the economies of scale given above are now somewhat out of date—for example the study reported by Maclean and Haigh was made 15 years ago. The experience of building larger process units which has been obtained since these estimates were made has extended the range of economies. The estimate of the economies of scale over the range 5 to 10 million tons given in table 5.5, and possibly in table 5.7, may therefore be on the low side. On the other hand the experience of building many small-scale refineries has resulted in developments which have reduced the capital and operating costs of small refineries of about 1 million tons capacity. An example of these developments is the prefabrication and skid-mounting of whole process units, thus avoiding expensive fabricating operations on the site. Another development has been the simplification of small refineries. The use of equipment which has long been taken for granted in constructing large-scale refineries has been questioned, and in some cases eliminated. This simplification is achieved at the expense of some loss of flexibility and a limitation of the range of products made.

The cost of crude, which is not included in the above estimates of operating costs, is likely to be affected by the scale of a refinery if this affects the size of tanker which can serve it, or alternatively, if large tankers serve a small refinery, by additional costs of storage. As we have seen above, refinery costs for a refinery with a capacity of 5 million tons represent about 20 per cent of the ex-refinery cost of refined products, and although the economies of scale of refineries are large in relation to refinery operating costs alone, they are much less significant in relation to total ex-refinery costs.

Table 5.9. Refinery and ex-refinery costs and scale

Crude input capacity (mn. tons)	Refinery costs (1)	Ex-refinery costs (2)
1	100	100
2	85	96
5	66	91
10	52	87

(1) See table 5.7.

(2) It is assumed that the costs of crude and works fuel are not affected by the level of throughput.

For the estimates of the economies of scale for refineries referred to above it was assumed that the smaller refineries were scaled-down versions of the larger refineries. This assumption has enabled us to estimate costs per ton of 'standardised' output, (1) but it exaggerates the economies of large refineries as it would not necessarily be economic for small refineries to include some process units. Apart from having different process units (and partly because of this) a small refinery may refine a crude oil with a different structure, produce a different product mix, and have less flexibility. One estimate of the economies of scale we obtained from an oil company gave the reduction in costs for a refinery with ten million tons, compared with a refinery with one million tons, as about 30 per cent of the costs of the smaller refinery for those products which the small refinery produced. This compares with the 48 per cent shown in table 5.9. Such estimates are particularly hazardous, however, because of the problem of joint costs.

So far we have only considered refineries with up to 10 million tons capacity, i.e. one-fifth of total U.K. refinery capacity in 1962. Larger refineries have been built—for example, the refinery at Abadan has a capacity

(1) i.e. total output arrived at by weighing the output of each product by an appropriate 'standard value'. In fact, in these estimates there has been no need to make this calculation because different refineries have heen assumed to have the same pattern of output.

of over 20 million tons. Even above an output of 10 million tons, there would still be some scope for technical economies of scale. These economies would be achieved by the use of larger units for some types of process and for offsite equipment. However, other factors such as the size of markets and the availability of utilities, of space for refinery expansion, and for tankers, limit the size of refineries in practice. Also the duplication of refineries reduces possible losses arising from a single fire or power failure.

Some comparisons of the costs of refining for U.S. refiners have been made by W. L. Nelson and described in various articles in the Oil and Gas Journal. These indicate that there may be some important additional qualifications to the estimates so far given. In practice Nelson found that there were significant differences between the costs of small- and large-scale refining companies. He found that small refiners, in terms of total refining capacity in one or more refineries, tend to operate equivalent refineries with less labour and to build plants at lower cost than the large refiners. Nelson suggested that 'the small-scale management has many inherent advantages such as freedom from committees, ease with which decisions can be shared between operators and management, ease with which responsibility can be defined, rapidity with which decisions can be formed, freedom in some degree from criticism by society and the possibility of intimate friendship and confidence between management and the refinery operators.'(1) The intensive efforts of the major oil companies to cut their costs in recent years, and the increased use of automatic instruments, computers and linear programming may have reduced these differences.

To what extent has a large refinery a marketing advantage? Clearly marketing economies of scale apply to companies rather than individual refineries. In the motor spirit, paraffin and household fuel markets, advertising on a national scale would be very expensive for a small refiner. In these markets important advantages also accrue to the first companies in the market as they are able to tie up many of the best selling sites. However, in markets for other products the power of advertising is a less potent force, and the smaller refiner can attempt to compete on price. In any case, marketing as opposed to delivery costs for these industrial markets are relatively unimportant.

Structure of the industry, and conclusions

How are these estimates of economies of scale reflected in the actual structure of the industry? Table 5.10 shows the crude distillation capacity of U.K. refineries in 1953 and 1962. Over 90 per cent of refinery capacity is owned by three companies, and the policy of these companies has clearly been to increase the scale of their refineries rather than build additional smaller-scale refineries. Both Shell and B.P., however, operate refineries with only 180,000 tons capacity. In the case of the British Petroleum Company, the Pumpherston refinery was built to re-

---

(1) W. L. Nelson. The Oil and Gas Journal. 23rd March 1959.

Table 5.10. Crude oil distillation capacity of U.K. refineries

Company	Refinery	Capacity in 1953 (mn. tons)	Capacity in 1962 (mn. tons)	Per cent of total capacity in 1962
Esso Petroleum	Fawley	7,200	11,500	22.2
	Milford Haven	—	4,800	9.3
	Total	7,200	16,300	31.5
Shell	Shell Haven	3,350	8,050	15.5
	Stanlow	4,550	6,000	11.6
	Haysham	1,800	1,800	3.5
	Ardrossan	—	180	0.3
	Total	9,700	16,030	30.9
B.P.	Kent	4,000	9,500	18.3
	Llandarcy	4,000	3,300	6.4
	Grangemouth	2,500	3,250	6.3
	Pumpherston	180	180	0.3
	Total	10,680	16,230	31.3
Mobil Oil	Coryton	873	2,373	4.6
Berry Wiggins & Co. Ltd.	Kingsnorth	69	195	0.4
	Weaste	56	168	0.3
	Total	125	363	0.7
Lobitos Oilfields Ltd.	Ellesmere Port	115	400	0.8
Manchester Oil Refinery Ltd.	Barton	125	150	0.3
Wm. Briggs & Son Ltd.	Dundee	37	60	0.1
	U.K. Total	28,855	51,906	100.0

Source: Ministry of Power Statistical Digest 1963.

fine locally produced shale oil, later supplemented by indigenous crude oil, and Shell's Ardrossan refinery is a specialised refinery for making bitumen which is mostly used for road works in Scotland. Most of the independent small refineries were first built in the 1930's and produce a limited range of products.

As expected, this study has shown that there are important economies of scale in this industry. Technical economies of scale appear to continue indefinitely with increasing size, and unit refinery operating costs fall substantially over the range of capacity from one to ten million tons. If we assume that small refineries are scaled-down versions of large refineries, unit refinery operating costs fall by about 50 per cent over this range of output. In terms of total ex-refinery costs, however, these economies are much smaller—of the order of 13 per cent. If the assumption that the smaller refineries are scaled-down versions of large ones is dropped the economies are reduced, but are still substantial.

In spite of these significant technical economies of scale, small refineries are in special circumstances economic. The main forces which contribute to this result are transport costs, historical factors—once a small refinery has been built the diseconomies of scale must be very considerable for it to be economic to close it down—and special factors such as a protected local source of crude or specialised high-value products.

A study of the economies of scale for the oil-refining industry is of particular interest at the present time because of the changing structure of the U.K. industry. As we have seen, refinery capacity in this country has up to now been dominated by a few large groups, and much the same has applied to the marketing of oil. A number of new entrants to the industry have appeared in recent years, and some of these are now planning to build refineries. In future there will be more competition, but there is clearly a danger that this will be bought at the expense of economies of scale.

6   Conclusions

Single-product plants

One of the objects of our research has been to assess the validity of the assumptions held by economists about the relationship between costs per unit of output and scale of production. Traditionally economists have tended to think in terms of single product plants when discussing economies of scale, and it seems worthwhile to start a review of our conclusions with a brief consideration of such plants, even though single-product plants do not in practice exist in the industries we have studied.

For plants set up to manufacture a single product in any of the four industries studied, substantial economies of scale would exist. On the basis of the equipment and techniques in use, the main economies of scale in the book-printing industry would result from the spreading of first copy costs and the use of high-capacity printing presses, and in the footwear industry from dividing and balancing operations and the use of specialist machinery. In the steel- and oil-refining industries the main economies would be achieved by the use of larger units of capital equipment, and, in some instances, particularly in the steel industry, by incorporating techniques in larger plants which are not economic for plants of smaller size.

Is there any output beyond which further economies of scale for single product plants are negligible? In all four industries studied the rate of decline of costs diminishes as scale increases and at some level of output the economies which would be achieved by further expansion would be small. For book printing the significance of spreading first copy costs inevitably falls rapidly as output rises and there are limits to the capacity of printing presses. Similarly in the footwear industry the scope for specialisation and balancing of operations declines, and the output capacity of the tools at present used in the industry is limited. Our estimates for the production of a standardised range of steel products and for oil refining, while indicating very substantial economies of scale, also show declining economies as output rises, indicating that the advantages to be derived from using equipment with larger dimensions falls. However, if market conditions had not prevented the construction of large-capacity single-product plants in all these industries, new techniques might well have been developed which would have extended the range over which economies of scale apply.

In the past it has been suggested that the costs of management may act as a diseconomy of scale, but we should not expect that this would be important in a plant producing one product. The costs of management would be relatively insignificant, as the control of such a plant would be straight-forward and there would be a limited range of production decisions for management to take. An exception to this general rule might occur in an industry in which the performance of individual operatives needed expert supervision, since it might be difficult in a very large plant to ensure good supervision.

Multi-product plants

A consideration of single-product plants is of little practical interest as most plants make a range of products. For multi-product plants there are, as we have seen, a number of inter-related dimensions of scale which have to be considered for a full assessment of the economies of scale. We discuss these dimensions of scale separately below.

1. The number of products produced

The economies of scale achieved in any plant with a given total output depend on the number of different products produced. The smaller the number, the greater the economies of scale. The clearest example of the economies of scale associated with large outputs of individual products are provided by book printing. (1) The first copy costs of composition vary inversely with the number of copies printed. Similar economies apply to the production of a new style of footwear, but the 'first copy' costs are of less significance in this industry and they are to some extent flexible in relation to the number of pairs of a style to be made. For steel production and oil refining the spreading of development costs of new products are not so important.

The production of a range of different products increases the problems of management and control and reduces the scope for achieving economies by using specialist machinery and by dividing and balancing operations. The effect on costs of the production of a range of products is particularly important in shoe production. Many firms in that industry make a range of styles which change as fashions in footwear evolve. The effect of this on the economies of scale is discussed in detail in the chapter on the footwear industry.

2. Production runs

Given the annual output of any particular product in a multi-product plant, the costs of producing that product may depend greatly on the number of production runs employed to produce that annual output. Short production runs involve frequent change-over and therefore higher costs. The clearest numerical example of the effect on costs of varying the length of production runs that we found was provided by book-printing. (2) For the book-printing industry, the economies of long production runs are achieved by reducing unit make-ready cost—the costs of setting up

---

(1) p. 29, p. 36.

(2) p. 29.

machines for a printing order. Though the measurement of the economies of long production runs is more difficult for footwear production, these economies appear to be of greater significance than for book-printing. Make-ready costs are negligible, but the speed and quality of work increases with the length of production runs, and long runs facilitate the balancing of operations and ease the problems of management, supervision and control. Economies of long production runs also apply in the steel industry. Offsetting the savings of long production runs in any industry are the costs of storing finished products and the losses incurred if some of the products cannot be sold, or can only be sold at a lower price than expected.

3. Production lines

For the footwear industry another dimension of scale is the number of separate production lines within a plant. By increasing the number of these lines it is possible to increase the degree of specialisation for individual operatives. Where production runs are short, or the diversity of styles marked, a number of lines can aid the balancing of operations. The fact that many departments of shoe factories have more than one production line indicates that the division of production lines is economically advantageous in these circumstances.

4. The overall output of plants

The number of products produced, the length of production runs, and the number of production lines, must be viewed in relation to the overall output of the plant. A large plant will enable a variety of products to be produced while achieving an efficient scale for each one. With given variety, the greater the output of a plant the greater the economies that can be grasped.

Another dimension of scale which affects the relationship between the overall output of a plant and costs is the number of operations performed. For example, in the footwear industry small factories tend to omit some operations, such as the cutting of soles for shoes, which larger factories perform themselves, and buy soles from specialist suppliers. In the circumstances the price paid by small plants for bought-out products is often comparable to the costs incurred by larger firms.

In other cases where the range of operations changes with scale we have encountered difficulty in making precise comparisons. For example, small steelworks and oil refineries may produce a different range of products from large plants and use different operations. They may even use different raw materials. For instance, a small steelworks may smelt scrap only and a small refinery may process only one particular type of crude oil. There are two approaches to measuring the economies of scale in such cases. Either costs for different scales of plant can be compared individually—e.g. the costs for a small steelworks using scrap only and for a large integrated steelworks converting iron ore—or one can compare the costs of producing a standardised pattern of output on different scales, even though this is an abstraction from reality.

We have chosen to estimate the relationship between costs and scale for plants with a standardised output and a given set of techniques, but we have attempted in addition to describe the consequences of varying these assumptions. These problems of different output patterns at different scales affect steel and oil particularly, and we have commented on it in the relevant chapters.

What are the technical factors which give rise to economies of scale in multi-product plants? Apart from the spreading of indivisible first-copy costs over a larger output as scale increases, the main sources of economies of scale for large plants are the use of larger capacity equipment, the use of more specialised equipment and personnel, and the greater utilisation of specialised resources by improving the balance of operations.

Examples of the effect of the use of larger units of equipment are provided by the relationship between costs and size for electric-arc furnaces and distillation units. Examples of the impact on costs of using equipment incorporating different techniques is provided by a comparison of hand and press clicking of shoes, and a comparison between costs and scale for four types of steel rolling mill.

The production of footwear involves a great many separate operations, and our study of this industry provided the clearest example of the effect of balancing operations. We also found that there was scope for balancing equipment and the output of operatives with special skills in the book-printing industry. In the steel and oil-refining industries items of plant can more readily be built to balance each other, but this may of course be achieved by some items being built with a capacity below that necessary to achieve the maximum economies of scale for individual items of plant.

We have found in all four industries that the average cost curve is L-shaped, in the sense that economies of scale tail off as output increases. However, these estimates are based on costs for plants of the size usually considered by businessmen in this country, and are therefore subject to the actual constraints imposed by the market. If these were removed new techniques and processes might be devised, particularly in the steel and oil-refining industries, to increase and extend the economies of scale at the upper end of the range.

Multi-plant firms

The main potential sources of economies of scale for multi-plant firms are the provision of specialist services and savings in selling and transport costs. However it is not possible to be categorical about the importance of these economies. Specialist services and the fruits of research can often be bought out. Selling costs often represent a very small proportion of total costs, as for book printers and steel producers, and potential disadvantages can be avoided by selling to merchants or large chains of shops, as in the footwear industry. The economies of large-scale advertising are of some importance in the footwear and oil industries, and here large firms do possess an advantage.

Another possible advantage of multi-plant firms is that they can specialise at each plant. Partly for historical reasons, and because of limitations on the supply of labour in a particular area, large firms often divide production between a series of plants each specialising in a limited range of products. If the market demands a wide range of products, a single-plant firm might have to have an uncomfortably large plant, from the labour and managerial points of view, if it is to produce the requisite variety on a large scale.

A possible disadvantage of multi-plant firms is that they may experience management difficulties. These can be avoided to some extent by delegation and by specialisation at each individual plant. The individual plants of multi-plant firms in the four industries we studied usually make separate products, and the problems of co-ordination are therefore limited, but problems of control nevertheless exist.

It is well known that large (usually multi-plant) firms can often obtain finance on cheaper terms than smaller firms. They can also obtain other advantages from their large overall size. We have not investigated these questions in detail for the purposes of this paper, which concentrates on technical economies. We believe that in many instances, however, technical economies are by far the most important cost-saving benefits derived from large-scale.

The significance of our conclusions

We have been impressed in the course of our research by the sheer diversity of the firms operating within each of the industries we have studied. The products which firms nominally in the same industry make, the age and type of equipment used, the apparent levels of efficiency, all vary widely. This has confirmed our original decision not to make use of comparative data for different firms, or time series data for particular plants, to estimate the economies of scale. Instead we have relied upon hypothetical engineering production functions. We believe that this method provides us with a reasonable measure of the technical economies of scale, but are inevitably much less sure of its usefulness when estimating the relationship between non-technical factors—e.g. the efficiency of management—and scale.

The implications of our conclusions for industrial efficiency are fairly clear. Substantial economies usually relate to the scale of output of individual products, and where scale is increased by widening the range of products technical economies may be small. This is perhaps the main reason why small-scale producers very often endeavour to produce goods whose special appeal to consumers is great enough to counteract the adverse effects on their prices of high costs due to small scale. Our estimates show that there are often substantial economies to be achieved by standardising production, by increasing the output of particular products, and by extending production runs. These conclusions may seem obvious, but the extent to which there is in practice a lack of standardisation and concentration of production suggests that they are worth stressing.

The significance of our conclusions for merger policy, or for State-inspired rationalisation, depends to some extent on the value put on the virtues of competition, since the maximum economies of scale may not be compatible with the existence of more than a relatively small number of firms in certain industries. In addition, the advantages or otherwise of rationalisation through mergers or State action may differ considerably in the short- or long-run. It may for example be true that, if one were starting with a clean slate, one would build less than a dozen integrated steelworks to produce all the steel that is required for home and export purposes in this country. In practice, however, one is not starting with a clean slate. Old works exist which may be able to earn a profit, over direct costs and inescapable overheads, for a long time to come, even when market prices are fixed on the basis of the total costs (including profit) of a modern large-scale plant. In these circumstances a rationalisation policy ought to move step by step if the lowest costs over time are to be achieved. It may be desirable, to begin with, simply to increase the length of runs in individual plants, or to arrnge for different plants to specialise more narrowly than they have been able to do in the past. The actual shutting down of complete plants may not at first be economic. Clearly no detailed conclusions regarding the means by which lowest costs can in practice be achieved in an industry can be arrived at without a detailed examination of the existing structure of that industry, including a consideration of the age of its plant and equipment. We have given some consideration to these questions in the individual industry chapters, but have only been able to do so to a limited extent.

Table 6. 1 shows our estimates of the minimum optimum scale for plants in the four industries we have studied, in terms both of absolute size and of the proportion of capacity in the United Kingdom represented by a plant of minimum optimum size i.e. the smallest size compatible with the lowest possible costs.

For the book-printing and footwear industries the conflict between economies of scale and competition does not occur to a marked extent, since printing houses and shoe factories, each with a representative product range, can obtain the full economies of scale with only 1-2 per cent of each industry's output capacity. Although printing houses and footwear factories specialise there is some flexibility, so that economies of scale do not preclude the possibility of a good deal of competition. Multi-plant firms in these industries may obtain some advantages, such as the economies of longer production runs, but these advantages are not likely to affect costs enough to be competitively decisive.

For bulk steel production, a relatively large share of total industry capacity is required to achieve the full economies of scale. For steel finishing operations the proportion of industry output required for the attainment of the full technical economies of scale varies according to the products made, but for the important sheet steel products a very high proportion of the industry's output is required. For oil refining, an output representing 17 per cent of the national output capacity is required to achieve most of the technical economies of scale for a refinery. Where the refinery serves a regional market its percentage of this market would of course be higher.

Table 6.1. Relationship between minimum optimum size of plant and
industry output

	Size of plant	Percentage of Total U.K. industry capacity in 1964
Book printing	300-400 Employees	1-2
Footwear	4,800 pairs a day	1-2
Bulk Steel Production	2 mn tons a year	7
Sheet Steel Production	3 " " " "	50
Oil Refining	10 " " " "	17

Note: The estimates in this table are made on the basis of certain
assumptions regarding 'product-mix' and, where appropriate,
length of product run etc. in each plant. The estimates would be
appreciably altered if very different assumptions about product-
mix etc. had been made. This is brought out clearly in the chapters
on individual industries. The estimates also assume shift-working
in steel and oil refining as normally practised, and that plant is
worked to capacity. The effect on costs of under-capacity working
is considered in the industry chapters.

Where there is a long-run conflict between the maintenance of competition and the full achievement of economies of scale, as there appears to
be in the steel and oil-refining industries, it is difficult to assess the
best compromise between scale and competition. As we have seen, it
is possible to make estimates of the economies of scale, but it would be
very difficult to assess the impact on the efficiency of an industry of the
presence or absence of competition. If the power of the State to influence
the structure of industries, either through exercising its purchasing
power or through its control over monopolies and restrictive practices,
is to be used effectively, difficult balancing problems are bound to arise.

Finally our studies have demonstrated the important contribution which
economies of scale may make when industries expand. These economies
are associated not only with the size of individual plants, but with the output of individual products and the length of production runs. These can be
increased when output increases. It may therefore be that the problem of
reconciling efficient scale with the maintenance of competition will be
eased in some industries as the market for their products expands. A
large market is however by itself no guarantee that a substantial proportion of output will be produced in plants of the minimum optimum scale.

UNIVERSITY OF CAMBRIDGE
DEPARTMENT OF APPLIED ECONOMICS

Occasional Papers

Papers already published

1 White-Collar Redundancy: A Case Study

By Dorothy Wedderburn

Mrs Wedderburn's case study is that of the dismissals which followed the cancellation of the defence contract for the Blue Water Guided Missile at the Luton and Stevenage factories of English Electric Aviation Ltd.

She first describes how the management dealt with the problem of bringing about a sharp and large reduction in the labour force, and then investigates what were the experiences and attitudes of the dismissed men, how long it took them to find jobs and what sort of jobs they found. It concludes with a brief discussion of possible lessons to be learned from the experience.

2 Railway Workshops: The Problems of Contraction

By P. Lesley Cook

In September 1962 a major plan for the contraction and reorganization of the main workshops of British Railways was announced. This plan proposed a reduction in the staff from 62,000 to 40,000 by 1967, the closure of a number of the large workshops and considerable investment in modern layouts. Dr Cook was given special facilities to make an independent investigation of the factors which made such a plan necessary and the basis for the numerous decisions.

The problems of contraction when combined with reorganization and investment are complicated and present unfamiliar theoretical problems, particularly in connexion with the utilization of capacity, the timing of action and the length of the time horizon which must be considered. The problems are not peculiar to the railway workshops and much of the discussion is of general application. The planning involved difficult choices as to which works should be retained and which men made redundant; the whole question of the social responsibilities of industry for easing the hardships of unemployment and redundancy is raised in an acute form. The conflicts between social responsibilities towards individuals and localities and the objective of efficiency and low costs had to be resolved.

4   Redundancy and the Railwaymen

By Dorothy Wedderburn

This is a study of the social consequences of the closure of railway workshops. Two workshops were selected for study, one at Gorton, Manchester—an area of relatively high employment—and one at Faverdale, Darlington—already scheduled as a Development District and with more workshop closures to come. Mrs Wedderburn describes how the workers dismissed—men with specialised skills, with long service in the workshop, whose fathers before them were often railwaymen—set about the task of finding new jobs. She and her team investigate how quickly the men found jobs, what sort of jobs they were and whether they had to move to find work; the crucial importance of the nation-wide economic expansion in 1964 becomes vividly apparent, as do the special problems of the men over sixty and others who have physical disabilities. They also investigate how the men adjusted socially, psychologically and economically to the change, and how far the arrangements made by the British Railways Board for handling the redundancy facilitated the change for the men.

This paper—which is a sequel to Mrs Wedderburn's earlier study White Collar Redundancy—should be of great value to Ministers and officials, business men and trade union leaders, students of economics and sociology, and indeed all who are concerned with one of today's leading problems.

5   Parking Space for Cars: Assessing the Demand

By C. J. Roth

Many city authorities are faced with two urgent and related problems: how many parking-spaces to provide, and what to charge for them.

In this paper Mr Roth reports on three pioneer attempts by the Department of Applied Economics, Cambridge, to assess the demand for parking space at various price-levels, made in the towns of Cambridge, Luton and Liverpool respectively. The account reveals many of the problems inherent in making the necessary surveys and analysing the results: it concludes that a combination of methods is needed to give the best guidance.

Some of the interesting quantitative conclusions concern the amount of potential demand which is now "frustrated" (because motorists do not take their cars into the city for fear of difficulty in finding a parking space), and the extent to which various levels of parking charge affect the demand.

This paper should be of great value to all who are concerned about
parking problems, and more especially to those who have to make quantitative decisions about the facilities to be provided and the prices to
be charged. No amount of data about the consequences of different
policies can, of itself, answer the political questions involved, but without the data, no rational decisions can be taken.

6   Wage Trends, Wage Policies and
Collective Bargaining

THE PROBLEMS FOR UNDER-DEVELOPED COUNTRIES

By H.A. Turner

This paper is based on Professor Turner's experience over a period
of some five years as a consultant to the Governments of various under-
developed countries or to the International Labour Organisation. It
considers how far the problems of wage-fixation in under-developed
countries are or are not similar to those in advanced countries, and
what the implications are for policy-making bodies.